Level 2

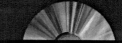

Nonfiction Comprehension
Test Practice

CD included

Correlated to State Standards

High-interest stories from TIME For Kids

Author
Jennifer Overend Prior, M.Ed.
Introduction by Kathleen Lewis, M.A.

Project Developer
Edward Fry, Ph.D.

Reading Passages provided by *TIME For Kids* magazine

SHELL EDUCATION

Editors
Karen Tam Froloff
Wanda Kelly, M.A.

Editorial Project Manager
Lori Kamola, M.S.Ed.

Editor-in-Chief
Sharon Coan, M.S.Ed.

Cover Artist
Neri Garcia

Illustration
Bruce Hedges

Product Manager
Phil Garcia

Publisher
Corinne Burton, M.A.Ed.

Shell Education
5301 Oceanus Drive
Huntington Beach, CA 92649-1030
http://www.shelleducation.com
ISBN-978-1-4258-0423-7
© *2006 Shell Educational Publishing, Inc.*
Reprinted 2013

Table of Contents

(**Note:** Each six-part lesson revolves around an article from *Time For Kids*. The article titles are listed here for you to choose topics that will appeal to your students, but the individual articles do not begin on the first page of the lessons. The lessons in this book may be done in any order.)

Standards Correlations

Shell Educational Publishing is committed to producing educational materials that are research- and standards-based. In this effort we have correlated all of our products to the academic standards of all 50 states, the District of Columbia, and the Department of Defense Dependent Schools. You can print a correlation report customized for your state directly from our website at **http://www.shelleducation.com.**

Purpose and Intent of Standards

The No Child Left Behind legislation mandates that all states adopt academic standards that identify the skills students will learn in kindergarten through grade twelve. While many states had already adopted academic standards prior to NCLB, the legislation set requirements to ensure the standards were detailed and comprehensive.

Standards are designed to focus instruction and guide adoption of curricula. Standards are statements that describe the criteria necessary for students to meet specific academic goals. They define the knowledge, skills, and content students should acquire at each level. Standards are also used to develop standardized tests to evaluate students' academic progress.

In many states today, teachers are required to demonstrate how their lessons meet state standards. State standards are used in development of all of our products, so educators can be assured they meet the academic requirements of each state. Complete standards correlation reports for each state can be printed directly from our website as well.

How to Find Standards Correlations

To print a correlation report for this product visit our website at **http://www.shelleducation.com** and follow the on-screen directions. If you require assistance in printing correlation reports, please contact Customer Service at 1-877-777-3450.

Graphic Development

Directions: Look at the map. Answer "True" (T) or "False" (F).

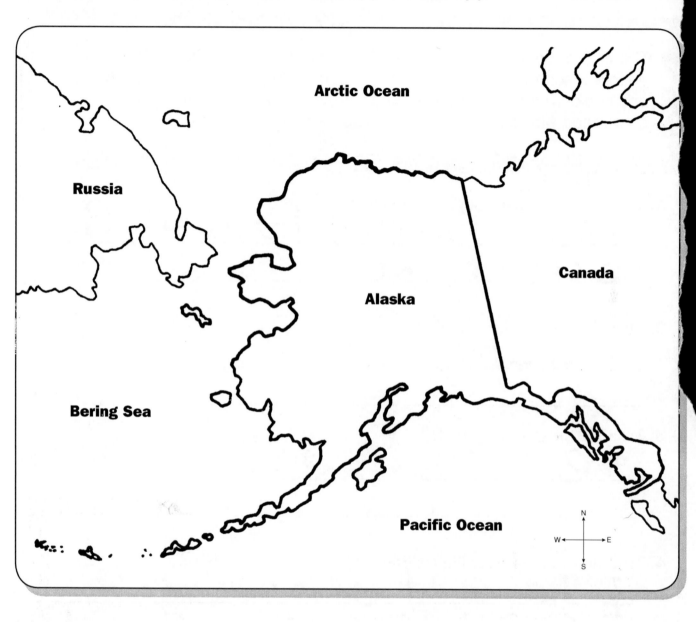

1. The Arctic Ocean is north of Alaska. _____

2. Russia touches Alaska. _____

3. Alaska is beside Canada. _____

4. The Pacific Ocean is south of Alaska. _____

5. Alaska is an island. _____

Enrichment

Directions: Read the information below and answer the following questions.

The Inupiat people live in Alaska. They live in small villages. The older people teach the children. The boys learn to hunt. The girls learn to sew and cook. The Inupiat people hunt for moose, whale, duck, and fish. They share food with each other. They also trade with families in their tribe.

1. How do the Inupiat people help each other?

They share food with each other.

2. How do they get their food?

hunting.

3. What do the girls learn to do?

sew and cook.

4. How do you think your life is different from Inupiat children?

I have tectnolage tv and a groshree shop.

5. Which food of the Inupiat would you like to try? Why?

non because i dont eat meat!

Name _____   Date _____

Paragraph Comprehension

Directions: Read the paragraph below and answer the following questions.

> The platypus is a mammal. It has hair and feeds milk to its babies. But it is like a bird in some ways. It has webbed feet. It also has a bill. Most mammal babies are born alive. But the platypus lays eggs.

1. A platypus is like a bird because

    a. it has webbed feet.

    b. it has a bill.

    c. it lays eggs.

    d. all of the above

2. Most mammal babies

    a. are born alive.

    b. can breathe underwater.

    c. are hatched from eggs.

3. The platypus

    a. lays eggs.

    b. gives birth to live babies.

    c. does not have babies.

4. What other animal has a bill?

    a. a shark

    b. a bird

    c. a lizard

    d. a dog

5. How do you think webbed feet help an animal?

    a. in swimming

    b. in running

    c. in eating

Name _____ Date _____

Sentence Comprehension

Directions: Read the following sentences carefully and answer the questions below "True" (T) or "False" (F).

> A platypus is a mammal. It has hair and feeds milk to its babies.

1. A platypus has feathers. _____f_____

2. A platypus can have babies. _____t_____

3. A platypus feeds milk to its babies. _____t_____

4. A platypus is an animal. _____t_____

5. A platypus is a person. _____f_____

Word Study

Directions: Read the definition and then answer the questions "yes" or "no."

> **mammal**
>
> an animal that breathes air, feeds milk to its babies, and has hair

1. Is a bird a mammal? _____yes no_____

2. Is a person a mammal? _____yes_____

3. Does a fish breathe air? _____no_____

4. Does a bird feed milk to its baby? _____yes no_____

5. Does a dog have hair? _____yes_____

Introduction

Why Every Teacher Needs This Book

In a day of increased accountability and standards-based instruction, teachers are feeling greater pressure for their students to perform well on standardized tests. Every teacher knows that students who can read, and comprehend what they read, will have better test performance.

In many classrooms today, teachers experience challenges they are not trained to meet, including limited English speakers, students with disabilities, high student mobility rates, and student apathy. Many states with poor standardized test scores have students who come from print-poor environments. Teachers need help developing competent readers and students who can apply their knowledge in the standardized test setting.

The *Nonfiction Comprehension Test Practice* series is a tool that will help teachers to teach comprehension skills to their students and enable their students to perform better in a test setting. This series supplies motivating, readable, interesting, nonfiction text, and comprehension exercises to help students practice comprehension skills while truly becoming better readers. The activities can be quick or in depth, allowing students to practice skills daily. What is practiced daily will be acquired by students. Practice for standardized tests needs to be started at the beginning of the school year, not a few weeks before the tests. The articles in this series are current and develop knowledge about today's world as well as the past. Students will begin thinking, talking, and developing a framework of knowledge which is crucial for comprehension.

When a teacher sparks an interest in knowledge, students will become life-long learners. In the process of completing these test practice activities, not only will you improve your students' test scores, you will create better readers and life-long learners.

Readability

All of the articles used in this series have been edited for readability. The Fry Graph, The Dale-Chall Readability Formula, or the Spache Readability Formula was used depending on the level of the article. Of more than 100 predictive readability formulas, these are the most widely used. These formulas count and factor in three variables: the number of words, syllables, and sentences. The Dale-Chall and Spache formulas also use vocabulary lists. The Dale-Chall Formula is typically used for upper-elementary and secondary grade-level materials. It uses its own vocabulary list and takes into account the total number of words and sentences. The formula reliably gives the readability for the chosen text. The Spache Formula is vocabulary-based, paying close attention to the percentage of words not present in the formula's vocabulary list. This formula is best for evaluating primary and early elementary texts. Through the use of these formulas, the levels of the articles are appropriate and comprehensible for students at each grade level.

Introduction (cont.)

General Lesson Plan

At each grade level of this series, there are 20 articles that prove interesting and readable to students. Each article is followed by questions on the following topics:

Sentence comprehension—Five true/false statements are related back to one sentence from the text.

Word study—One word from the text is explained (origin, part of speech, unique meaning, etc.). Activities can include completion items (cloze statements), making illustrations, or compare and contrast items.

Paragraph comprehension—This section contains one paragraph from the text and five multiple-choice questions directly related to that paragraph. The questions range from drawing information directly from the page to forming opinions and using outside knowledge.

Whole-story comprehension—Eight multiple-choice questions relate back to the whole article or a major part of it. They can include comprehension that is factual, is based on opinion, involves inference, uses background knowledge, involves sequencing or classifying, relates to cause and effect, or involves understanding the author's intent. All levels of reading comprehension are covered.

Enrichment for language mechanics and expression—This section develops language mechanics and expression through a variety of activities.

Graphic development—Graphic organizers that relate to the article are used to answer a variety of comprehension questions. In some lessons, students create their own maps, graphs, and diagrams that relate to the article.

The following is a list of words from the lessons that may be difficult for some students. These words are listed here so that you may review them with your students as needed.

Word	Page	Word	Page	Word	Page
Inupiat	21	sauropod	61	camouflage	109
Osborne	27	grizzly	63	gorillas	111
Titanic	29	Cleopatra	69	caused	119
medicines	33	Goddio	70	Nikolai	124
monarch	39	chores	82	Anchorage	125
mimicry	43	capitalize	85	apostrophe	127
platypus	45	skeleton	87	giraffe	131
Koorina	47	quilt	93	adjective	133
athlete	51	ancestors	94	Nunavut	137
Madagascar	57	Bengal	105	Inuit	137
prosauropods	61	Korku	105		

Introduction *(cont.)*

What Do Students Need to Learn?

Successful reading requires comprehension. Comprehending means having the ability to connect words and thoughts to knowledge already possessed. If you have little or no knowledge of a subject, it is difficult to comprehend an article or text written on that subject. Comprehension requires motivation and interest. Once your students start acquiring knowledge, they will want to fill in the gaps and learn more.

In order to help students be the best readers they can be, a teacher needs to be familiar with what students need to know to comprehend well. A teacher needs to know Bloom's levels of comprehension, traditional comprehension skills and expected products, and the types of questions that are generally used on standardized comprehension tests, as well as methods that can be used to help students build a framework for comprehension.

Bloom's Taxonomy

In 1956, Benjamin Bloom created a classification for questions that are commonly used to demonstrate comprehension. These levels are listed here along with the corresponding skills that will demonstrate understanding and are important to remember when teaching comprehension to assure that students have attained higher levels of comprehension. Use this classification to form your own questions whenever students read or listen to literature.

Knowledge—Students will recall information. They will show knowledge of dates, events, places, and main ideas. Questions include words such as: *who, what, where, when, list, identify,* and *name.*

Comprehension—Students will understand information. They will compare and contrast, order, categorize, and predict consequences. Questions include words such as: *compare, contrast, describe, summarize, predict,* and *estimate.*

Application—Students will use information in new situations. Questions include words such as: *apply, demonstrate, solve, classify,* and *complete.*

Analysis—Students will see patterns. They will be able to organize parts and figure out meaning. Questions include words such as: *order, explain, arrange,* and *analyze.*

Synthesis—Students will use old ideas to create new ones. They will generalize, predict, and draw conclusions. Questions include words such as: *what if, rewrite, rearrange, combine, create,* and *substitute.*

Evaluation—Students will compare ideas and assess value. They will make choices and understand a subjective viewpoint. Questions include words such as: *assess, decide,* and *support your opinion.*

Introduction (cont.)

Comprehension Skills

There are many skills that form the complex activity of comprehension. This wide range of understandings and abilities develops over time in competent readers. The following list includes many traditional skills found in scope and sequence charts and standards for reading comprehension.

identifies details

recognizes stated main idea

follows directions

determines sequence

recalls details

locates reference

recalls gist of story

labels parts

summarizes

recognizes anaphoric relationships

identifies time sequence

describes a character

retells story in own words

infers main idea

infers details

infers cause and effect

infers author's purpose/intent

classifies, places into categories

compares and contrasts

draws conclusions

makes generalizations

recognizes paragraph (text) organization

predicts outcome

recognizes hyperbole and exaggeration

experiences empathy for a character

experiences an emotional reaction to the text

judges quality/appeal of text

judges author's qualifications

recognizes facts vs. opinions

applies understanding to a new situation

recognizes literary style

recognizes figurative language

identifies mood

identifies plot and story line

Introduction (cont.)

Observable Comprehension Products

There are many exercises that students can complete when they comprehend the material they read. Some of these products can be performed orally in small groups. Some lend themselves more to independent paper-and-pencil type activities. Although there are more, the following are common and comprehensive products of comprehension.

Recognizing—underlining, multiple-choice items, matching, true/false statements

Recalling—writing a short answer, filling in the blanks, flashcard question and answer

Paraphrasing—retelling in own words, summarizing

Classifying—grouping components, naming clusters, completing comparison tables, ordering components on a scale

Following directions—completing steps in a task, using a recipe, constructing

Visualizing—graphing, drawing a map, illustrating, making a time line, creating a flow chart

Fluent reading—accurate pronunciation, phrasing, intonation, dramatic qualities

Reading Comprehension Questions

Teaching the kinds of questions that appear on standardized tests gives students the framework to anticipate and thus look for the answers to questions while reading. This framework will not only help students' scores, but it will actually help them learn how to comprehend what they are reading. Some of the types of questions students will find on standardized comprehension tests are as follows:

Vocabulary—These questions are based on word meaning, common words, proper nouns, technical words, geographical words, and unusual adjectives.

Facts—These questions ask exactly what was written, using *who, what, when, where, why, how,* and *how many.*

Sequence—These questions are based on order—what happened first, last, and in between.

Conditionals—These questions use qualifying terms such as: *if, could, alleged,* etc.

Summarizing—These questions require students to restate, choose main ideas, conclude, and create a new title. Also important here is for students to understand and state the author's purpose.

Outcomes—These questions often involve readers drawing upon their own experiences or bringing outside knowledge to the composition. Students must understand cause and effect, results of actions, and implications.

Opinion—These questions ask the author's intent and mood and require use of background knowledge to answer.

Introduction *(cont.)*

Graphic Organizers

Reading and comprehension can be easier for students with a few simple practices. For top comprehension, students need a wide vocabulary, ideas about the subject they are reading, and understanding of the structure of the text. Pre-reading activities will help students in all of these areas. Graphic organizers help students build vocabulary, brainstorm ideas, and understand the structure of the text.

Graphic organizers aid students with vocabulary and comprehension. Graphic organizers can help students comprehend more and, in turn, gain insight into how to comprehend in future readings. This process teaches a student a way to connect new information to prior knowledge that is stored in his or her brain. Different types of graphic organizers are listed below by category.

Graphic organizers include: semantic maps, spider maps (word webs), Venn diagrams, and fishbone diagrams.

Semantic map—This organizer builds vocabulary. A word for study is placed in the center of the page, and four categories are made around it. The categories expand on the nature of the word and relate it back to personal knowledge and experience of the students.

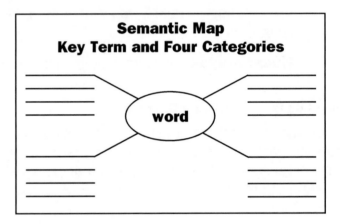

Spider map (word web)—The topic, concept, or theme is placed in the middle of the page. Like a spider's web, thoughts and ideas come out from the center, beginning with main ideas and flowing out to details.

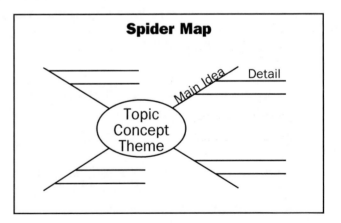

Introduction (cont.)

Graphic Organizers (cont.)

Venn diagram—This organizer compares and contrasts two ideas. With two large circles intersecting, each circle represents a different topic. The area of each circle that does not intersect is for ideas and concepts that are only true about one topic. The intersection is for ideas and concepts that are true about both topics.

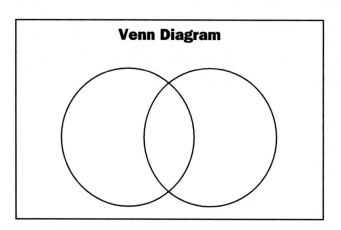

Fishbone diagram—This organizer deals with cause and effect. The result is listed first, branching out in a fishbone pattern with the causes that lead up to the result, along with effects that happened.

Continuum organizers can be linear or circular and contain a chain of events. These include time lines, chain of events, multiple linear maps, and circular or repeating maps.

Time lines—Whether graphing ancient history or the last hour, time lines help students see how events have progressed and understand patterns in history.

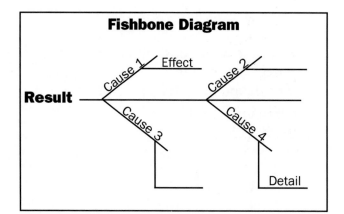

Introduction *(cont.)*

Graphic Organizers *(cont.)*

Chain of events—This organizer not only shows the progression of time but also emphasizes cause and effect. Beginning with the initiating event inside of a box, subsequent arrows and boxes follow showing the events in order.

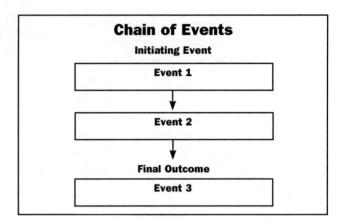

Multiple linear maps—These organizers can help students visualize how different events can be happening at the same time, either in history or in a story, and how those events affect each other.

Circular or repeating maps—These organizers lend themselves to events that happen in a repeating pattern like events in science, such as the water cycle.

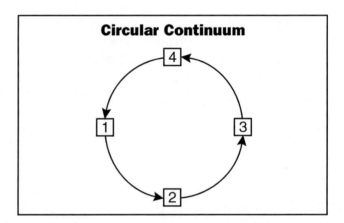

Hierarchical organizers show structure. These include network trees, structured overviews, and class/example and properties maps. These organizers help students begin to visualize and comprehend hierarchy of knowledge, going from the big picture to the details.

Network tree—This organizer begins with a main, general topic. From there it branches out to examples of that topic, further branching out with more and more detail.

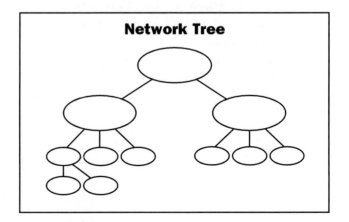

Introduction *(cont.)*

Graphic Organizers *(cont.)*

Structured overview—This is very similar to a network tree, but it varies in that it has a very structured look.

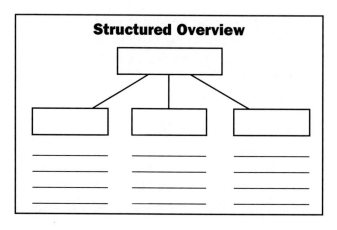

Class/example and properties map—Organized graphically, this map gives the information of class, example, and properties.

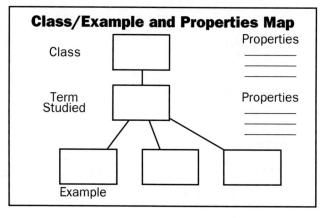

Spreadsheets are important organizers today. Much computer information is stored on spreadsheets. It is important for students to learn how to create, read, and comprehend these organizers. These include semantic feature analysis, compare and contrast matrices, and simple spreadsheet tables.

Semantic feature analysis—This organizer gives examples of a topic and lists features. A plus or a minus indicates if that example possesses those features.

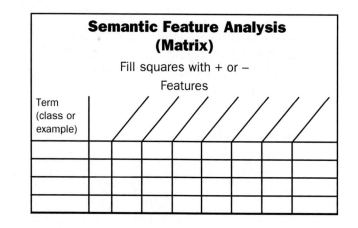

Introduction (cont.)

Graphic Organizers (cont.)

Compare and contrast matrix—This organizer compares and contrasts two or more examples are different attributes.

Compare/Contrast Matrix (Spreadsheets)		
Attribute 1		
Attribute 2		
Attribute 3		

Simple spreadsheet table—Much information can be visualized through spreadsheets or tables. Choose examples and qualities and arrange them in spreadsheet style.

Maps are helpful in understanding spatial relationships. There are geographical maps, but there are also street maps and floor plans.

Geographical map—These organizers can range from globes to cities, and details are limited.

Street map—Information on this type of organizer becomes more detailed.

Floor plan—This organizer becomes more detailed, from a building to a room or a student's desk.

Numerical graphs such as bar graphs, pie charts, and tables become important in comprehension, too.

Bar graph—With a vertical and horizontal axis, this graph shows a comparison between subjects. It is important to be able to draw the correct information out of it.

Pie chart—In the circular shape of a pie, amounts totaling 100% are shown as pieces of pie. Once again, drawing correct information is important.

Table—Information is organized into rows and columns to display relationships. A table can help to recognize patterns in a given problem.

Using graphic organizers while reading class material will help students know what to do in order to better comprehend material on standardized comprehension tests. Further, a varied use of all types of organizers will help students of different learning styles find a method that works for them.

Pre-reading Strategies

It is widely understood that for comprehension and acquisition to take place, new information must be integrated with what the reader knows. Pre-reading strategies will help students to build knowledge and restructure the information they already possess in order to more fully comprehend what they are reading. After a teacher has spent time teaching pre-reading strategies, students will know what to do when reading on their own.

Introduction (cont.)

Building Vocabulary

Common sense reveals that there is a symbiotic relationship between knowledge of vocabulary and comprehension. Vocabulary development and comprehension span the curriculum. Students come across a large and diverse vocabulary in science, social science, mathematics, art, and even physical education. Skills and strategies for understanding vocabulary can be taught throughout the day. You can build your students' vocabulary directly and/or indirectly. Both ways have shown merit for different learners, so a combination will be sure to help all of the learners in your classroom.

Whether done directly or indirectly, teaching the kind of vocabulary that occurs in a text will greatly improve comprehension. Teaching vocabulary directly, a teacher would list the vocabulary in the text and have the students find the definitions in some manner. Indirectly, a teacher would introduce the content of the text and then elicit vocabulary that the students bring with them on the subject. The use of graphic organizers is helpful in doing this. (See pages 10–14 for different types.) The teacher would lead the discussion to specific words if necessary.

Direct teaching—The more conventional way of teaching vocabulary has its merits. Give students a list of vocabulary words and they look them up. This way teaches the use of reference materials and for some learners it is a good way to learn vocabulary. However, students truly learn vocabulary when they are involved in the construction of meaning rather than simply memorizing definitions.

Incidental or indirect teaching—This is really a combination of direct teaching and incidental learning for the well-equipped teacher. Teaching in this fashion, a teacher uses the students' knowledge and interests to begin a vocabulary development session that will end with what he or she wants the students to learn. Along the way, the teacher builds a grand vocabulary list and student interest. Also, students buy into the fact that they are part of the process and that learning vocabulary can be a personal experience that they can control. The students will learn how to become independent learners, studying things that interest them.

A general approach to building vocabulary could include the following:

Semantic association—Students brainstorm a list of words associated with a familiar word, sharing everyone's knowledge of vocabulary and discussing the less familiar words.

Semantic mapping—Once the brainstorming is done, students can group the words into categories, creating a visual organization to understand relationships.

Semantic feature analysis—Another way to group words is according to certain features. Use a chart to show similarities and differences between words.

Analogies—This practice will further help students see the relationships of words. Also, analogies are often used on standardized tests. (e.g., Doctor is to patient as teacher is to student .)

Word roots and origins—The study of these, as well as affixes, will help students deduce new words. Students can ask themselves, "Does it look like a word I know? Can I figure out the meaning in the given context?"

Introduction (cont.)

Building Vocabulary (cont.)

Synonyms and antonyms—The study of these related words provides a structure for meaning and is also good practice for learning and building vocabulary.

Brainstorming—The use of graphic organizers to list and categorize ideas will help greatly with comprehension. A great way to get started is with a KWL chart. By listing ideas that are known, what students want to know, and, when finished, what they learned, relationships will be established so that comprehension and acquisition of knowledge will take place. Word webs work well, too. Anticipating the types of words and ideas that will appear in the text will help with fluency of reading as well as with comprehension.

Understanding Structure

To be able to make predictions and find information in writing, a student must understand structure. From the structure of a sentence to a paragraph to an essay, this skill is important and sometimes overlooked in instruction. Some students have been so immersed in literature that they have a natural understanding of structure. For instance, they know that a fairy tale starts out "Once upon a time . . . ," has a good guy and a bad guy, has a problem with a solution, and ends ". . . happily ever after." But when a student does not have this prior knowledge, making heads or tails of a fairy tale is difficult. The same holds true with not understanding that the first sentence of a paragraph will probably contain the main idea, followed with examples of that idea. When looking back at a piece to find the answer to a question, understanding structure will allow students to quickly scan the text for the correct area in which to find the information. Furthermore, knowing where a text is going to go structurally will help prediction as well as comprehension.

Building a large vocabulary is important for comprehension, but comprehension and acquisition also require a framework for relating new information to what is already in the brain. Students must be taught the structure of sentences and paragraphs. Knowing the structure of these, they will begin to anticipate and predict what will come next. Not having to decode every word reduces the time spent reading a sentence and thus helps students remember what they read at the beginning of the sentence. Assessing an author's purpose and quickly recalling a graphic or framework of personal knowledge will help a reader predict and anticipate what vocabulary and ideas might come up in an article or story.

Several activities will help with understanding structure. The following list offers some ideas to help students:

Write—A great way to understand structure is to use it. Teach students the proper structure when they write.

Color code—When reading a text, students can use colored pencils or crayons to color code certain elements such as main idea, supporting sentences, and details. Once the colors are in place, they can study and tell in their own words about paragraph structure.

 ©Shell Educational Publishing

Introduction *(cont.)*

Understanding Structure *(cont.)*

Go back in the text—Discuss a comprehension question with students. Ask them, "What kinds of words are you going to look for in the text to find the answer? Where are you going to look for them?" (The students should pick main ideas in the question and look for those words in the topic sentences of the different paragraphs.)

Graphic organizers—Use the list of graphic organizers (pages 10–14) to find one that will suit your text. Have students create an organizer as a class, in a small group, or with a partner.

Study common order—Students can also look for common orders. Types of orders can include chronological, serial, logical, functional, spatial, and hierarchical.

Standardized Tests

Standardized tests have taken a great importance in education today. As an educator, you know that standardized tests do not necessarily provide an accurate picture of a student. There are many factors that do not reflect the student's competence that sway the results of these tests.

- The diversity of our big country makes the tests difficult to norm.

- Students who are talented in areas other than math and language cannot show this talent.

- Students who do not speak and read English fluently will not do well on standardized tests.

- Students who live in poverty do not necessarily have the experiences necessary to comprehend the questions.

The list could go on, but there does have to be some sort of assessment of progress that a community can use to decide how the schools are doing. Standardized tests and their results are receiving more and more attention these days. The purpose of this series, along with creating better readers, is to help students get better results on standardized tests.

Test Success

The ability to do well when taking traditional standardized tests on comprehension requires at least three things:

- a large vocabulary of sight words

- the mastery of certain specific test-taking skills

- the ability to recognize and control stress

Vocabulary has already been discussed in detail. Test-taking skills and recognizing and controlling stress can be taught and will be discussed in this section.

Introduction (cont.)

Test-Taking Skills

Every student in your class needs good test-taking skills, and almost all of them will need to be taught these skills. Even fluent readers and extremely logical students will fair better on standardized tests if they are taught a few simple skills for taking tests.

These test-taking skills are:

- The ability to follow complicated and sometimes confusing directions. Teach students to break down the directions and translate them into easy, understandable words. Use this series to teach them the types of questions that will appear.
- The ability to scale back what they know and concentrate on just what is asked and what is contained in the text—show them how to restrict their responses. Question students on their answers when doing practice exercises and have them show where they found the answer in the text.
- The ability to rule out confusing distracters in multiple choice answers. Teach students to look for key words and match up the information from the text.
- The ability to maintain concentration during boring and tedious repetition. Use practice time to practice this and reward students for maintaining concentration. Explain to students why they are practicing and why their concentration is important for the day of the test.

There are also environmental elements that you can practice with throughout the year in order for your students to become more accustomed to them for the testing period.

If your desks are pushed together, have students move them apart so they will be accustomed to the feel on test-taking day.

- Put a "Testing—Do Not Disturb" sign on the door.
- Require "test etiquette" when practicing: no talking, attentive listening, and following directions.
- Provide a strip of construction paper for each student to use as a marker.
- Establish a routine for replacing broken pencils. Give each student two sharpened pencils and have a back-up supply ready. Tell students they will need to raise their broken pencil in their hand, and you will give them a new one. One thing students should not worry about is the teacher's reaction to a broken pencil.
- Read the instructions to the students as you would when giving a standardized test so they grow accustomed to your test-giving voice.

As a teacher, you probably realize that what is practiced daily is what is best learned. All of these practices work well to help students improve their scores.

Introduction (cont.)

Reduce Stress and Build Confidence

As well as the physical and mental aspects of test-taking, there is also the psychological. It is important to reduce students' stress and increase students' confidence during the year.

- In order to reduce stress, it first needs to be recognized. Discuss feelings and apprehensions about testing. Give students some tools for handling stress.

- Begin talking about good habits at the beginning of the year. Talk about getting enough sleep, eating a good breakfast, and exercising before and after school. Consider sending home a letter encouraging parents to start these good routines with their children at home.

- Explain the power of positive thought to your students. Tell them to use their imaginations to visualize themselves doing well. Let them know that they have practiced all year and are ready for what is to come.

- Remember to let students stretch and walk around between tests. Try using "Simon Says" with younger students throughout the year to get them to breathe deeply, stretch, and relax so it won't be a novel idea during test time.

- Build confidence during the year when using the practice tests. Emphasize that these tests are for learning. If they could get all of the answers right the first time, they wouldn't need any practice. Encourage students to state at least one thing they learned from doing the practice test.

- Give credit for reasonable answers. Explain to students that the test makers write answers that seem almost true to really test the students' understanding. Encourage students to explain why they chose the answers they gave, and then reason with the whole class on how not to be duped the next time.

- Promote a relaxed, positive outlook on test-taking. Let your students know on the real day that they are fully prepared to do their best.

Introduction *(cont.)*

Suggestions for the Teacher

When practicing skills for comprehension, it is important to vocalize and discuss the process in finding an answer. After building vocabulary, tapping background knowledge, and discussing the structure that might be used in the article, have the students read the article. If they are not able to read the article independently, have them read with partners or in a small teacher-led group. After completing these steps, work through the comprehension questions. The following are suggestions for working through these activities:

- Have students read the text silently and answer the questions.

- Have students correct their own papers.

- Discuss each answer and how the students came to their answers.

- Refer to the exact wording in the text.

- Discuss whether students had to tap their own knowledge or not.

Answer Sheet

The teacher can choose to use the blank answer sheet located at the back of the book for practice filling in bubble forms for standardized tests. The rows have not been numbered so that the teacher can use the form for any test, filling in the numbers and copying for the class as necessary. The teacher can also have the students write the answers directly on the pages of the test practice sheets instead of using the bubble sheet.

CD-ROM

A CD-ROM with all the lessons, answer sheet, and answer key has been provided at the back of this book.

Summary

Teachers need to find a way to blend test preparation with the process of learning and discovery. It is important for students to learn test-taking skills and strategies because they will be important throughout life. It is more important for students to build vocabulary and knowledge, to create frameworks for comprehension, and to become fluent readers.

The *Nonfiction Comprehension Test Practice* series is an outstanding program to start your students in the direction of becoming better readers and test-takers. These are skills they will need throughout life. Provide an atmosphere conducive to the joy of learning and create a climate for curiosity within your classroom. With daily practice of comprehension skills and test-taking procedures, teaching comprehension may seem just a little bit easier.

Name _____ Date _____

Whole-Story Comprehension

Directions: Read the story below and answer the questions on the following page.

A Special Delivery

Hooray for Koorina! She is a platypus in Australia. She lives in a home for animals. In 1999, she became a mother. This is big news. Platypuses are wild animals. They only have babies when they are free. Koorina became the only platypus mom kept by people.

The platypus is a mammal. It has hair and feeds milk to its babies. But it is like a bird in some ways. It has webbed feet. It also has a bill. Most mammal babies are born alive. But the platypus lays eggs.

Koorina hid her tiny new babies in a nest. When they were older, she brought them out. Everyone was happy to see them.

Whole-Story Comprehension (cont.)

Directions: After you have read the story on the previous page, answer the questions below.

1. Koorina

    a. lives in the wild.

    b. is kept by people.

    c. is a baby.

2. Why is it strange that a platypus has a bill?

    a. It's like a zebra.

    b. It's like a bird.

    c. It's like a turtle.

3. Koorina lives

    a. with other animals.

    b. alone.

    c. in China.

4. Koorina is the only platypus kept by people to

    a. have webbed feet.

    b. have hair.

    c. have a baby.

5. Where did Koorina keep her babies?

    a. in a cage

    b. in the water

    c. in a pouch

    d. in a nest

6. Why couldn't people see the babies when they hatched?

    a. She hid them.

    b. They were too small.

    c. They ran away.

7. Which of the following is not a mammal?

    a. a cat

    b. a fish

    c. a person

    d. a whale

8. Everyone was

    a. afraid of the babies.

    b. happy to see the babies.

    c. trying to find the babies.

Enrichment

Directions: Read the information given in the box. Rewrite each sentence below. Add at least one adjective.

Adjectives are words that describe. They make a story interesting.

Here is an example:

Platypuses are wild animals.

Wild is an adjective. It describes animal.

---

1. She is a platypus in Australia.

_____

_____

2. It has webbed feet.

_____

_____

3. Most mammal babies are born alive.

_____

_____

4. Koorina hid her babies in a nest.

_____

_____

Graphic Development

Directions: Use the picture and what you have read to complete the chart.

Mammal Characteristics	Non-mammal Characteristics

Sentence Comprehension

Directions: Read the following sentence carefully and answer the questions below "True" (T) or "False" (F).

> A baseball team needs bats, but not bats with wings.

1. Baseball bats have wings on them. _____

2. A bat is used to play baseball. _____

3. A bat is an animal. _____

4. Bats can fly. _____

5. Flying bats play baseball. _____

Word Study

Directions: Read the definitions. Then, write "A" or "B" to tell which definition is being used in each sentence.

> **bat**
>
> A. a metal or wooden object used for hitting a ball
>
> B. a flying animal

_____ **1.** The athlete broke his bat.

_____ **2.** Bats sleep during the day.

_____ **3.** My dad gave me a new bat.

_____ **4.** I hit better with this bat.

_____ **5.** A bat came out of the cave.

_____ **6.** Bats eat bugs.

Paragraph Comprehension

Directions: Read the paragraph below and answer the following questions.

> A baseball team needs bats, but not bats with wings. The New York Mets had 30,000 of them hanging around. In spring 1998, a colony of bats moved into the stadium in Florida. This is where the Mets practice in the spring.

1. Who are the New York Mets?

    a. bats

    b. scientists

    c. a baseball team

2. Do baseball bats have wings?

    a. yes

    b. no

    c. sometimes

3. What problem did the Mets have?

    a. Bats moved into their stadium.

    b. Their bats were broken.

    c. They lost too many games.

4. Where do the Mets practice in the spring?

    a. in New York

    b. in a bat cave

    c. in Florida

5. A colony is

    a. a group of bats.

    b. a group of baseball players.

    c. a place to play sports.

ARTICLE FROM

TIME
FOR KIDS

Name _____ Date _____

Whole-Story Comprehension

Directions: Read the story below and answer the questions on the following page.

To the Bat House!

A baseball team needs bats, but not bats with wings. The New York Mets had 30,000 of them hanging around. In spring 1998, a colony of bats moved into the stadium in Florida. This is where the Mets practice in the spring.

Why did the bats move into a stadium? Bats usually live in forests. Buildings have replaced their homes. A wildlife expert explains, "Bats now have to live close to people."

"Too close," said the Mets. The bats were making a big mess. Bat droppings were piling up. The stadium was starting to stink! The bats had to go. Nets were put up to keep them out. A special bat house was built nearby. Now the bats have a new home base!

Name _____   Date _____

Whole-Story Comprehension *(cont.)*

Directions: After you have read the story on the previous page, answer the questions below.

1. What happened to the bats' real homes?

   a. They were crowded.

   b. They were destroyed.

   c. They were too dirty.

2. What happens when bats' homes disappear?

   a. They move closer to people.

   b. They become pets.

   c. They hide underground.

3. Why are the droppings a problem?

   a. They stink.

   b. They make a mess.

   c. both a and b

4. How many bats were in the stadium?

   a. hundreds

   b. thousands

   c. millions

5. A wildlife expert

   a. knows a lot about nature.

   b. knows a lot about baseball.

   c. is a kind of animal.

6. What was used to keep the bats out?

   a. baseball bats

   b. traps

   c. nets

7. What did they do with the bats?

   a. They sold them as pets.

   b. They built them a bat house.

   c. They took them to another country.

8. What is a bat house?

   a. A baseball stadium.

   b. It is a special place for bats.

   c. It is a place for putting baseball bats.

Name _____ Date _____

Enrichment

Directions: Read the information in the box below and then complete the activity. Read the following sentences. Then write "fact" or "opinion" to identify what type of sentence it is.

> A **fact** is something that is true.
>
> *Bats are animals.*
>
> An **opinion** tells the way someone feels about something.
>
> *I like bats.*

1. Bats are scary. _____

2. Bats fly. _____

3. Some bats have lost their homes. _____

4. Bats are ugly. _____

5. Bats live in groups. _____

6. Bats live in Florida. _____

7. Some people hate bats. _____

8. Bats usually live in forests. _____

Name _____   Date _____

Graphic Development

Directions: Bats have different kinds of noses. Some bats are named because of their noses. Look carefully at each of the bats' noses and then write their correct names on the lines below.

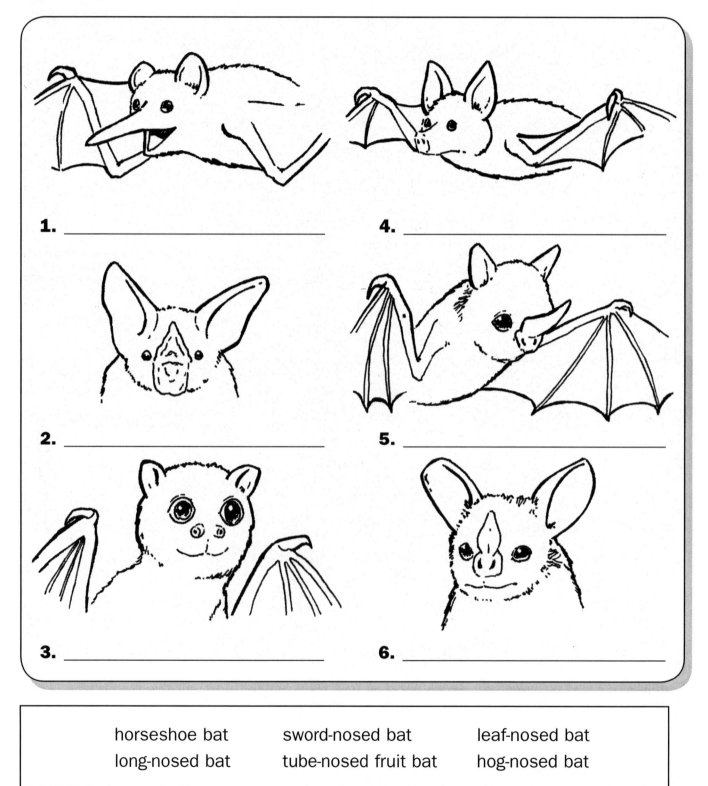

1. _____

2. _____

3. _____

4. _____

5. _____

6. _____

| horseshoe bat | sword-nosed bat | leaf-nosed bat |
| long-nosed bat | tube-nosed fruit bat | hog-nosed bat |

Sentence Comprehension

Directions: Read the following sentences carefully and answer the questions below "True" (T) or "False" (F).

> They were digging on an island. It is called Madagascar. It is near Africa.

1. Madagascar is an island. _____

2. People were digging on the island. _____

3. The island is near Africa. _____

4. Africa is near Madagascar. _____

5. The island is called Africa. _____

Word Study

Directions: Read the definition below and then answer the questions.

dinosaur

terrible lizard or marvelous lizard

1. What kind of animal was a dinosaur (bird, mammal, reptile)?

_____

2. Why do you think they are called *terrible* and *marvelous*?

_____

Name _____ Date _____

Paragraph Comprehension

Directions: Read the paragraph below and answer the following questions.

> Dinosaurs died many years ago. But when did they first show up? In 1999, scientists learned something new.

1. Dinosaurs

    a. are alive today.

    b. live in zoos.

    c. lived many years ago.

2. Scientists don't know

    a. when dinosaurs first showed up.

    b. anything about dinosaurs.

    c. where to look for dinosaurs.

3. What happened to the dinosaurs?

    a. They are hiding.

    b. They found new homes.

    c. They died.

4. Some scientists

    a. study dinosaurs.

    b. keep dinosaurs in cages.

    c. try to find live dinosaurs.

5. Scientists

    a. learn new things about dinosaurs.

    b. don't know about dinosaurs.

    c. don't want to learn about dinosaurs.

ARTICLE FROM
TIME
FOR KIDS

Name _____ Date _____

Whole-Story Comprehension

Directions: Read the story below and answer the questions on the following page.

The Very First Dinosaur?

Dinosaurs died many years ago. But when did they first show up? In 1999, scientists learned something new.

They were digging on an island. The island is called Madagascar. It is near Africa. They found the jaws of two new dinosaurs. They learned a lot from the jaws. The animals had small heads. They had long necks. They ate plants. They were the size of kangaroos. They walked on four legs.

The bones tell even more. These dinosaurs lived two million years before any other dinosaur!

Name _____ Date _____

Whole-Story Comprehension (cont.)

Directions: After you have read the story on the previous page, answer the questions below.

1. Why were the scientists digging?

    a. They were looking for dinosaurs.

    b. They were looking for jewels.

    c. They were making sand castles.

2. The dinosaurs they found had

    a. big heads.

    b. flat heads.

    c. small heads.

3. The parts they found were

    a. the jaws.

    b. the teeth.

    c. the noses.

4. The dinosaurs were bigger than

    a. dogs.

    b. horses.

    c. elephants.

5. These dinosaurs

    a. crawled.

    b. walked on two legs.

    c. walked on four legs.

6. They ate

    a. meat.

    b. plants.

    c. both meat and plants.

7. These dinosaurs could be

    a. the last ones that died.

    b. the very first dinosaurs.

    c. the smallest dinosaurs.

8. Scientists can tell how old they are by

    a. their color.

    b. their size.

    c. their bones.

Name _____ Date _____

Enrichment

Directions: Read the information and then answer the questions.

> The bones found on Madagascar were from dinosaurs called prosauropods. *Sauropod* means lizard-footed. *Prosauropod* means before the sauropod.

1. Why do you think these dinosaurs were called *lizard-footed*?

_____

_____

_____

2. Which came first, the sauropod or the prosauropod?

_____

_____

_____

Name _____ Date _____

Graphic Development

Directions: Use the map to answer the questions.

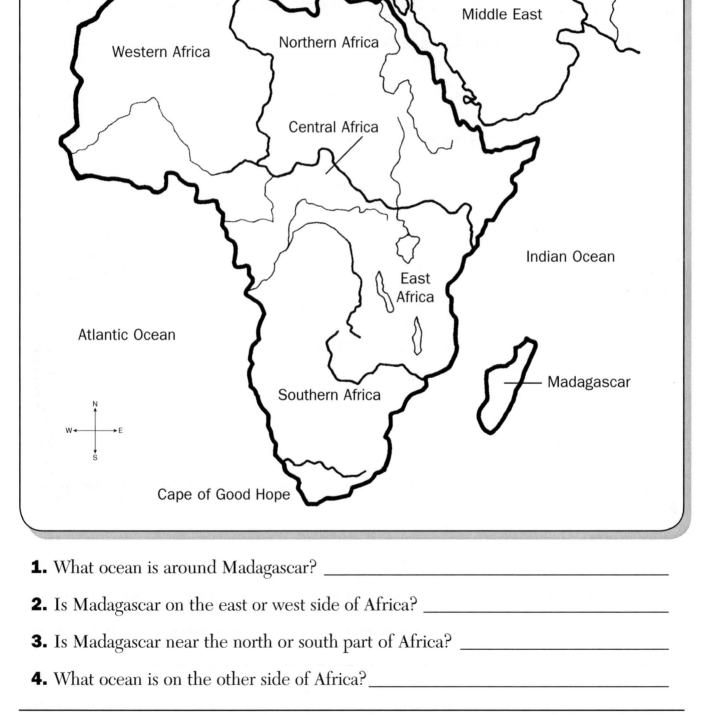

1. What ocean is around Madagascar? _____

2. Is Madagascar on the east or west side of Africa? _____

3. Is Madagascar near the north or south part of Africa? _____

4. What ocean is on the other side of Africa?_____

Sentence Comprehension

Directions: Read the following sentences carefully and answer the questions below "True" (T) or "False" (F).

> In 1975, a law was passed to help bears. People could not hurt them. They could not tear down their homes.

1. The bears' homes are protected. _____

2. Sometimes people hurt bears. _____

3. People probably hurt bears because they fear them. _____

4. Some people want to help grizzly bears. _____

5. No one wants to help bears. _____

• •

Word Study

Directions: Read the information below and then answer the question.

> **Yellowstone National Park**
>
> Yellowstone was named a national park in 1872. It was meant to be a place for people to enjoy. Nature is left alone there. Animals and plants are protected.

How does Yellowstone National Park help endangered animals?

_____

_____

_____

_____

Paragraph Comprehension

Directions: Read the paragraph below and answer the following questions.

> Once there were many grizzly bears in the United States. Later, they were in danger. There weren't many left. In 1975, a law was passed to help bears. People could not hurt them. They could not tear down their homes.

1. Why did people tear down bears' homes?

   a. to build them new ones

   b. to get rid of them

   c. to help them

2. Another word for *in danger* is

   a. endangered.

   b. extinct.

   c. healthy.

3. Government wanted to

   a. get rid of bears.

   b. kill bears.

   c. help bears.

4. The new law helped bears by

   a. protecting their homes.

   b. keeping them from harm.

   c. both a and b

5. Why do you think people fear bears?

   a. They think they are dangerous.

   b. They think they are ugly.

   c. They think they will take their food.

ARTICLE FROM
TIME
FOR KIDS

Name _____ Date _____

Whole-Story Comprehension

Directions: Read the story below and answer the questions on the following page.

The Bears Bounce Back

Once there were many grizzly bears in the United States. Later, they were in danger. There weren't many left. In 1975, a law was passed to help bears. People could not hurt them. They could not tear down their homes.

The plan is working. Today, there are many more bears. Most of them live in Yellowstone National Park. Sometimes bears go outside of the park. They may kill sheep or cows. Some people are afraid. They want to shoot a bear that might harm them. Other people say there aren't enough bears. They say we should keep helping them. Everyone hopes people and bears can learn to live together.

Name _____ Date _____

Whole-Story Comprehension (cont.)

Directions: After you have read the story on the previous page, answer the questions below.

1. Did the law help bears?

   a. yes

   b. no

   c. It is too soon to tell.

2. Where do most of the bears live?

   a. in zoos

   b. in Arizona

   c. in Yellowstone National Park

3. Why are some people afraid of the bears now?

   a. They sometimes leave the park.

   b. They kill sheep and cattle.

   c. both a and b

4. Why do some people want to shoot bears?

   a. They want to protect themselves.

   b. They want to eat their meat.

   c. They want their fur.

5. Some people say

   a. there are too many bears.

   b. there aren't enough bears.

   c. bears should be extinct.

6. A national park

   a. is a safe place for bears.

   b. is not safe for bears.

   c. is like a zoo.

7. In a national park, bears can

   a. roam free.

   b. stay in cages.

   c. be caught in traps.

8. The government thinks that people should

   a. learn to live near bears.

   b. keep bears as pets.

   c. kill bears.

Enrichment

Directions: Read the information and then complete the activity.

When two words are put together to make one word, it is called a **compound word**.

Look at the words below. Put the words together to make compound words.

1. some + times = _____

2. out + side = _____

3. every + one = _____

4. Yellow + stone = _____

5. to + day = _____

Now try to form three more compound words.

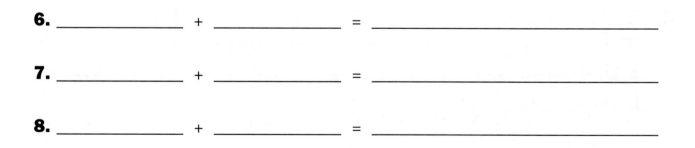

6. _____ + _____ = _____

7. _____ + _____ = _____

8. _____ + _____ = _____

Graphic Development

Directions: Use the map to answer the questions.

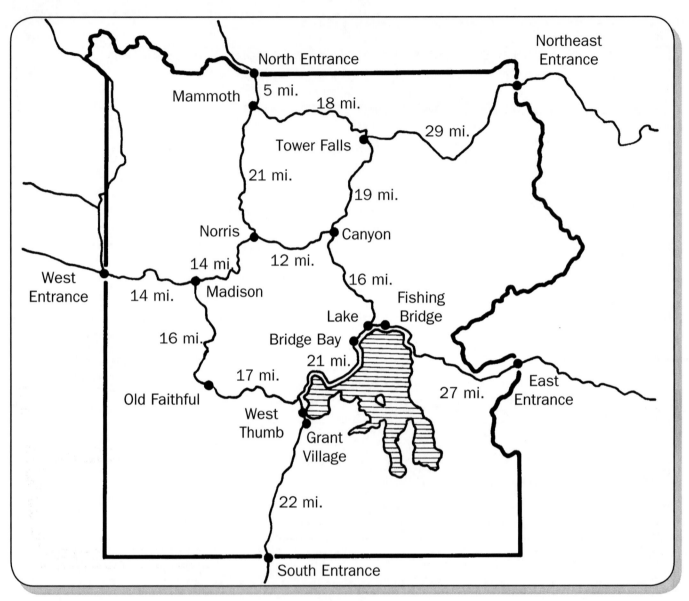

1. How many miles is it from Mammoth to Norris? _____

2. How far is it from the West Entrance to Old Faithful? _____

3. Name two places that are on the lake. _____

4. How far is it from the South Entrance to Bridge Bay? _____

5. How many miles is it from the North Entrance to the South Entrance? (Choose any path you want.) _____

Sentence Comprehension

Directions: Read the following sentences carefully and answer the questions below "True" (T) or "False" (F).

> Cleopatra was the last queen of Egypt. She was only 17 years old!

1. Egypt used to have a queen. _____

2. Egypt has a queen now. _____

3. Egypt's last queen was an old woman. _____

4. Cleopatra was young. _____

5. Cleopatra was a boy. _____

Word Study

Directions: Read the information. Underline each proper noun. Write "person," "place," or "thing" below the sentence.

> A **noun** is a person, a place, or a thing.
>
> A **proper noun** is the name of a person, a place, or a thing.

1. The diver was Franck Goddio.

_____

2. He found it in a city in Egypt.

_____

3. Cleopatra was the last queen.

_____

Paragraph Comprehension

Directions: Read the paragraph below and answer the following questions.

The diver was Franck Goddio. He found the statue near a city in Egypt. There was an old palace there. It is now under water. It has been under water for many, many years. It belonged to Cleopatra. She was a queen.

1. What did the diver find?

    a. a statue

    b. Cleopatra

    c. Egypt

2. Cleopatra was

    a. a diver.

    b. a queen.

    c. a king.

3. The city is

    a. on a hill.

    b. in a valley.

    c. under water.

4. This diver

    a. swims under water.

    b. dives off of a diving board.

    c. jumps out of an airplane.

5. The statue he found was

    a. new.

    b. old.

    c. broken.

Name _____ Date _____

Whole-Story Comprehension

Directions: Read the story below and answer the questions on the following page.

Underwater Treasures

A diver found a rock in the water. He cleaned it off. It turned out to be a very old statue.

The diver was Franck Goddio. He found the statue near a city in Egypt. There was an old palace there. It is now under water. It has been under water for many, many years. It belonged to Cleopatra. She was a queen.

Cleopatra was the last queen of Egypt. She was only 17 years old! The city of Rome took over Egypt. That's why she was Egypt's last queen.

Many people want to know more about her story. Goddio wants to build an underwater museum near the old palace.

Whole-Story Comprehension (cont.)

Directions: After you have read the story on the previous page, answer the questions below.

1. Egypt used to have

    a. an underwater city.

    b. divers.

    c. a queen.

2. Cleopatra was a queen when she was

    a. 17 years old.

    b. a baby.

    c. an old woman.

3. Egypt was taken over by

    a. Rome.

    b. Cleopatra.

    c. the ocean.

4. What does Goddio want to build?

    a. a statue

    b. a palace

    c. an underwater museum

5. Why does Goddio want to build a museum?

    a. to hide the statue

    b. to show people the underwater city

    c. so only he can go there

6. What did the diver first think the statue was?

    a. a rock

    b. a palace

    c. a queen

7. Many people want to know

    a. where the palace is.

    b. more about Cleopatra.

    c. how to dive.

8. A museum is

    a. always in the water.

    b. only in Egypt.

    c. a place to show valuable objects.

Enrichment

Directions: Read the information below and then answer the questions using complete sentences.

> A long time ago, many places had kings and queens. A king or a queen would rule over the people. They made decisions for the people. If a king died, his son or daughter would be the next king or queen. The people could not decide who would rule over them.

1. Do we have a king or queen in the United States?

_____

_____

2. Who is the leader of our country?

_____

_____

3. How is that person chosen to lead us?

_____

_____

4. Did people vote for a king or queen years ago?

_____

_____

Graphic Development

Directions: Use the map to answer the questions.

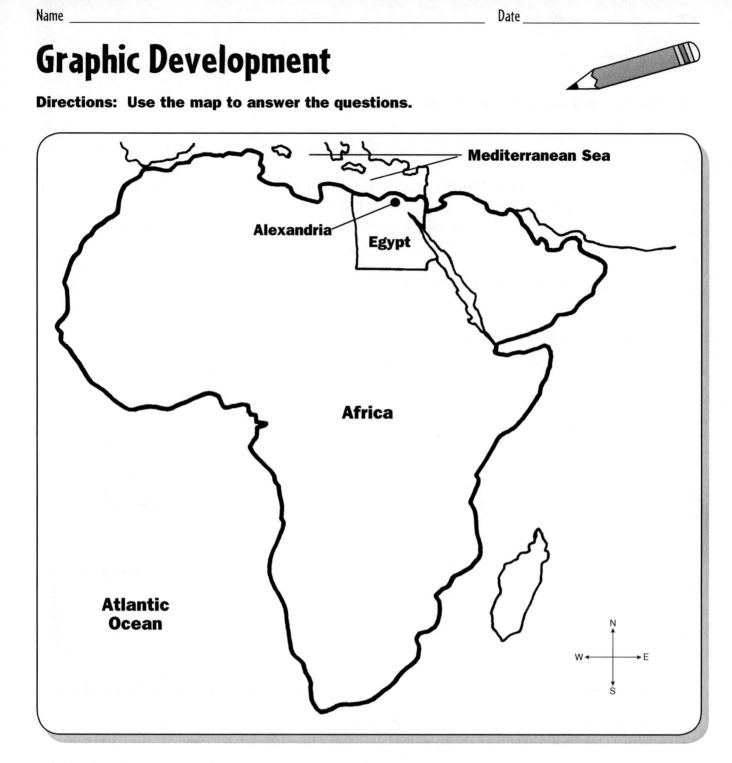

1. Egypt is on what continent? _____

2. The underwater city was found in Alexandria. In what country is Alexandria?

_____

3. Is Egypt in the north, south, east, or west in Africa? _____

4. What body of water is beside Alexandria? _____

Sentence Comprehension

Directions: Read the following sentence carefully and answer the questions below "True" (T) or "False" (F).

I think it is wrong to kill animals and eat them.

1. The person in this sentence eats meat. _____

2. Some people don't like to eat meat. _____

3. People kill animals for food. _____

4. The person in this sentence probably thinks no one should ever eat meat. _____

5. Some people think it is wrong to kill animals. _____

• •

Word Study

Directions: Read the definition and then answer the questions.

vegetarian

a person who does not eat meat

1. Name two reasons why you think vegetarians don't eat meat.

_____

_____

2. What kinds of foods do you think a vegetarian eats?

_____

_____

Paragraph Comprehension

Directions: Read the paragraph below and answer the following questions.

The school lunch menu should change. I am a vegetarian. This means that I do not eat meat. All the lunches at school have meat in them. This is not fair.

1. This person does not eat meat because

    a. she is a vegetarian.

    b. meat makes her feel sick.

    c. she doesn't like the taste.

2. A vegetarian will probably eat

    a. fruit.

    b. vegetables.

    c. both a and b

3. What problem does the girl have?

    a. She isn't healthy.

    b. She can't eat school lunches.

    c. She doesn't like school.

4. The person says

    a. she might just eat the meat.

    b. it isn't fair.

    c. she doesn't have to go to school.

5. What does the girl want?

    a. to bring her own lunch

    b. to go to a restaurant for lunch

    c. to have the school change the lunch menu

ARTICLE FROM TIME FOR KIDS

Name _____ Date _____

Whole-Story Comprehension

Directions: Read the letter below and answer the questions on the following page.

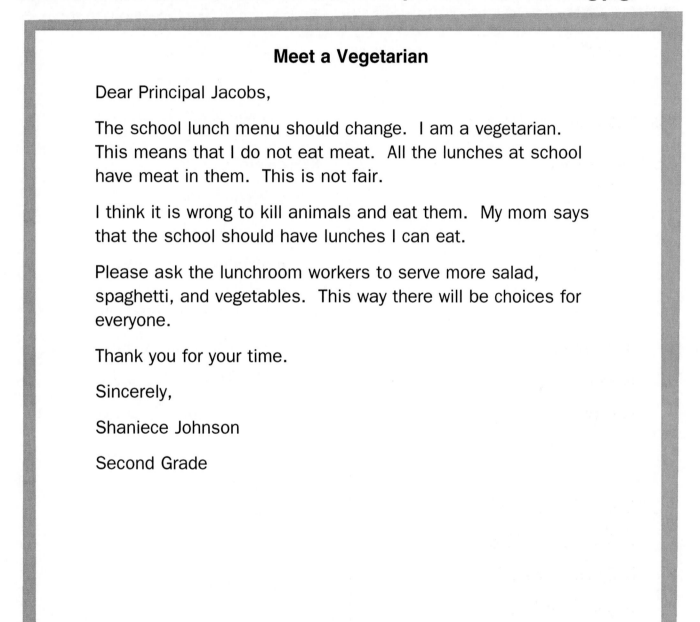

Meet a Vegetarian

Dear Principal Jacobs,

The school lunch menu should change. I am a vegetarian. This means that I do not eat meat. All the lunches at school have meat in them. This is not fair.

I think it is wrong to kill animals and eat them. My mom says that the school should have lunches I can eat.

Please ask the lunchroom workers to serve more salad, spaghetti, and vegetables. This way there will be choices for everyone.

Thank you for your time.

Sincerely,

Shaniece Johnson

Second Grade

Whole-Story Comprehension *(cont.)*

Directions: After you have read the previous page, answer the questions below.

1. This writing is in the form of

    a. a letter.

    b. a story.

    c. a play.

2. It is written to

    a. a teacher.

    b. a friend.

    c. a principal.

3. The girl is

    a. happy.

    b. upset.

    c. excited.

4. The girl wants the principal to

    a. eat the school lunches.

    b. cook the school lunches.

    c. ask the workers to change the lunches.

5. She would like the school to serve

    a. more meat.

    b. more sandwiches.

    c. more spaghetti and vegetables.

6. The girl is in

    a. second grade.

    b. high school.

    c. sixth grade.

7. At the end of the letter, the girl

    a. says the menu should change.

    b. thanks the principal.

    c. explains that she is a vegetarian.

8. She hopes that the school will give children

    a. more choices.

    b. more chicken.

    c. a longer recess.

Enrichment

Directions: Label the parts of a letter (greeting, message, closing) on the lines provided.

1. _____ [Dear Kayla,

2. _____ [I want to know if you would like to come to my house today after school. We could call your mom at lunchtime to ask her. I think we would have a lot of fun. I have neat toys to play with.

3. _____ [Your friend,

Cindy

Graphic Development

Directions: Look at the food pyramid. Plan a healthy meal for a vegetarian. Remember not to include meat.

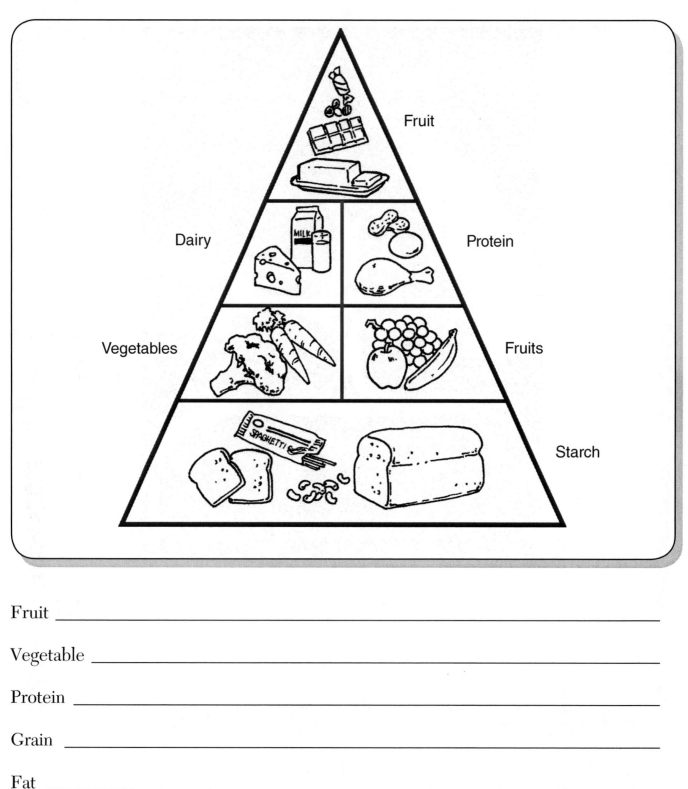

Fruit _____

Vegetable _____

Protein _____

Grain _____

Fat _____

Sentence Comprehension

Directions: Read the following sentences carefully and answer the questions below "True" (T) or "False" (F).

> Please raise my allowance by 50 cents a week. I think I should get more money.

1. This girl already gets an allowance. _____

2. The girl wants more money. _____

3. The girl thinks she already has a lot of money. _____

4. The girl is probably writing to her friend. _____

5. The girl wants to get a raise. _____

Word Study

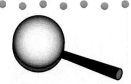

Directions: Read the definitions. Then, write "A" or "B" to tell which definition is being used in each sentence.

> **raise**
>
> A. to lift up
>
> B. to increase

_____ **1.** Please raise your hand.

_____ **2.** Raise the pencil off your paper.

_____ **3.** The boss gave the man a raise.

_____ **4.** I would like a raise in my allowance.

Paragraph Comprehension

Directions: Read the paragraph below and answer the following questions.

> I have more chores than before. I promise to finish each of them. And I will sweep the porch every weekend, even if you don't ask me to.

1. In order to get more money, the girl will

   a. get mad.

   b. be nice to her sister.

   c. do more chores.

2. The girl is

   a. getting angry.

   b. begging.

   c. trying to convince.

3. The extra chore she will do is

   a. sweep the porch.

   b. clean her room.

   c. make dinner.

4. She promises to

   a. finish her chores.

   b. be nice.

   c. go to bed early.

5. A chore is

   a. homework.

   b. a job at home.

   c. a game.

Whole-Story Comprehension

Directions: Read the letter below and answer the questions on the following page.

May I Have a Raise?

Dear Mom and Dad,

Please raise my allowance by 50 cents a week. I think I should get more money. Here are my reasons:

1. I have more chores than before. I promise to finish each of them. And I will sweep the porch every weekend, even if you don't ask me to.

2. The price of snacks and school supplies has gone up. I need more money to pay for them.

Please think about these two reasons. Whatever you decide to do, remember that I think you are the best parents in the world!

Your daughter,

Emily

Whole-Story Comprehension (cont.)

Directions: After you have read the previous page, answer the questions below.

1. This writing is in the form of

    a. a story.

    b. an article.

    c. a letter.

2. The girl is writing to

    a. her mother.

    b. her father.

    c. both of her parents.

3. The snacks at school

    a. taste bad.

    b. cost more.

    c. are on sale.

4. Even if her parents don't ask, she will

    a. go to school on time.

    b. sweep the porch.

    c. do her homework.

5. She wants to buy

    a. snacks and supplies.

    b. clothes.

    c. games.

6. In her letter, she sounds

    a. angry.

    b. unhappy.

    c. polite.

7. The girl lists _____ reasons.

    a. one

    b. two

    c. three

8. If she doesn't get a raise, she will

    a. get a job.

    b. keep bothering them.

    c. still think her parents are great.

Enrichment

Directions: Read the information below and complete the activity. Write each closing correctly.

> There are many ways to close a letter. When you write a closing, you should capitalize the first (or only) word. You should not capitalize the second word.
>
> Here are some examples:
>
> Your friend,
>
> Sincerely,

1. your friend, _____

2. fondly, _____

3. your daughter, _____

4. sincerely yours, _____

5. yours truly, _____

6. truly yours, _____

Graphic Development

Directions: Think of something you would like to convince your parents of. Use the graphic organizer.

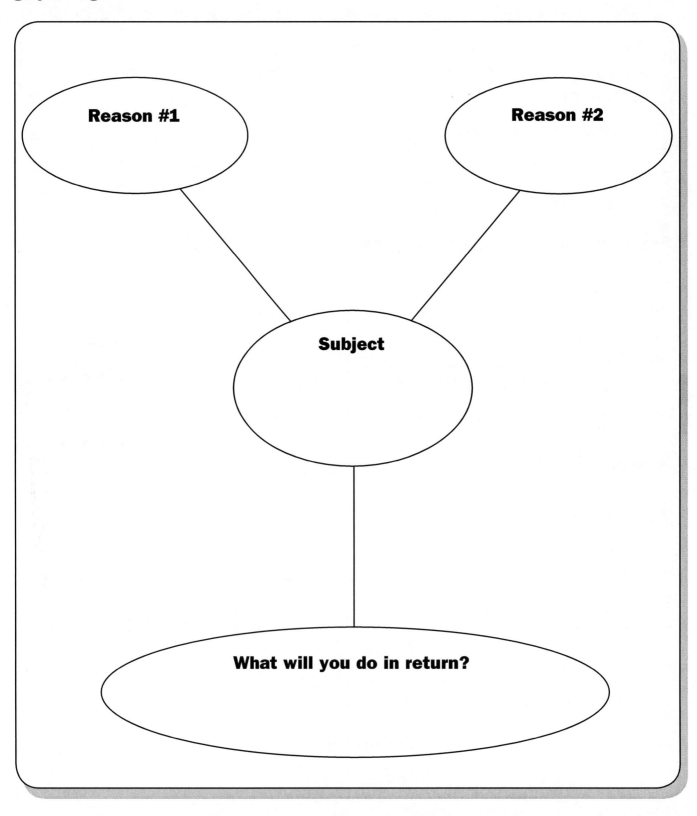

Name _____ Date _____

Sentence Comprehension

Directions: Read the following sentences carefully and answer the questions below "True" (T) or "False" (F).

> A boy looks at a skeleton in a glass case. There is a bullet in its leg.

1. A girl is looking in the case. _____

2. A boy sees a skeleton. _____

3. There is something strange about the skeleton. _____

4. The boy sees a bullet in the skeleton. _____

5. The bullet is in the skeleton's arm. _____

• •

Word Study

Directions: Read the definitions. Then, write "A" or "B" to tell which definition is being used in each sentence.

> **settle**
>
> A. to make a home
>
> B. to make quiet
>
> C. to make right

_____ **1.** Tell the children to settle down.

_____ **2.** When we got to the hotel, we settled in.

_____ **3.** The settlers moved to Jamestown.

_____ **4.** We settled our problem.

Paragraph Comprehension

Directions: Read the paragraph below and answer the following questions.

> Scientists know the man lived about 400 years ago. He lived in Jamestown, Virginia. Settlers from England landed there. They built a fort near the James River.

1. The man died

    a. last year.

    b. a month ago.

    c. a long time ago.

2. The man was a

    a. settler.

    b. doctor.

    c. hunter.

3. He probably came from

    a. Virginia.

    b. England.

    c. Jamestown.

4. What did the settlers live in?

    a. a house

    b. a tent

    c. a fort

5. They built their fort near

    a. a river.

    b. a lake.

    c. the ocean.

Name _____ Date _____

Whole-Story Comprehension

Directions: Read the story below and answer the questions on the following page.

The Mystery of Jamestown

A boy looks at a skeleton in a glass case. There is a bullet in its leg.

"What happened to this guy?" asks the boy. "What was his name?" No one really knows.

Scientists know the man lived about 400 years ago. He lived in Jamestown, Virginia. Settlers from England landed there. They built a fort near the James River.

Life was hard for them. Many died from sickness. Others died fighting the Spanish and Native Americans. By 1699, no one lived at the fort. Everyone thought it had washed away.

But not long ago scientists dug up the fort. They found many things. They found guns, pots, toys, and coins. These things are helping to solve the mystery of life in Jamestown.

Name _____ Date _____

Whole-Story Comprehension *(cont.)*

Directions: After you have read the story on the previous page, answer the questions below.

1. The boy wanted to know

    a. the man's name.

    b. what happened to him.

    c. both a and b

2. A settler is a person who

    a. sets things down.

    b. settles fights.

    c. moves somewhere to live.

3. How did many settlers die?

    a. They got sick.

    b. They were killed.

    c. both a and b

4. What did people think happened to the fort?

    a. It fell apart.

    b. It washed away.

    c. It was buried.

5. Which of the following were not found in the fort?

    a. pots

    b. guns

    c. blankets

6. Which of the following was found in the fort?

    a. coins

    b. knives

    c. clothes

7. The fort was found

    a. under ground.

    b. in a lake.

    c. in the river.

8. Scientists are trying to

    a. solve a mystery.

    b. rebuild the fort.

    c. find more forts.

Enrichment

Directions: Read the information in the box below and complete the activity. Read each sentence below. Write the correct form of the number on each line.

> When numbers are used in writing, use the written word for the number unless it is larger than the number nine.
>
> Here are some examples:
>
> I ate three donuts.
>
> My dad is 38 years old.

1. Scientists know the man lived _____ years ago.
(400, four hundred)

2. They found _____ pretty pots.
(3, three)

3. I have _____ old coins.
(5, five)

4. I bet there are _____ toys in that fort.
(100, one hundred)

Graphic Development

Directions: Use the map to answer the questions.

State	Location
Massachusetts	
Rhode Island	
Connecticut	
New Jersey	
Delaware	
Maryland	

Wisconsin

Michigan

New York

Pennsylvania

Iowa

Ohio

Illinois

Indiana

West Virginia

Virginia

Missouri

Kentucky

Tennessee

North Carolina

Atlantic Ocean

Arkansas

South Carolina

Alabama

Georgia

Florida

Louisiana

Mississippi

Gulf of Mexico

N
W ← → E
S

1. Virginia is near which ocean? _____

2. Name two states that are north of Virginia. _____

3. What state is directly south of Virginia? _____

Sentence Comprehension

Directions: Read the following sentences carefully and answer the questions below "True" (T) or "False" (F).

> A quilt is made of pieces of cloth. They are sewn together in a pattern.

1. A quilt is sewn together. _____

2. A quilt is made of one piece of cloth. _____

3. The sentences above say a quilt is used for dusting. _____

4. The cloth is sewn in patterns. _____

• •

Word Study

Directions: Read the information and then answer the question.

The Underground Railroad

A long time ago, there were black slaves in the South. Many of them tried to be free. They ran away from their owners. It was dangerous to run away. The Underground Railroad helped slaves get to the North. In the North they could be free. Many people helped slaves on their way to freedom.

What does it mean to you to be free?

_____

_____

_____

Paragraph Comprehension

Directions: Read the paragraph below and answer the following questions.

Ozella McDaniel Williams had a story to tell. She sold quilts in South Carolina. Her ancestors were slaves. She told this story about the Underground Railroad.

1. Ozella McDaniel Williams sold

    a. food.

    b. quilts.

    c. dresses.

2. People in her family were

    a. doctors.

    b. sailors.

    c. slaves.

3. She lived in

    a. South Carolina.

    b. North Carolina.

    c. Georgia.

4. She told a story about

    a. her quilts.

    b. South Carolina.

    c. the Underground Railroad.

5. A slave is a person who

    a. is owned by another person.

    b. has a job.

    c. doesn't have a house.

Name _____ Date _____

Whole-Story Comprehension

Directions: Read the story below and answer the questions on the following page.

Slaves' Secret Code

A quilt is made of pieces of cloth. They are sewn together in a pattern. History is like a quilt. It is made up of stories. One story can change the way we look at the past.

Ozella McDaniel Williams had a story to tell. She sold quilts in South Carolina. Her ancestors were slaves. She told this story about the Underground Railroad.

"The Railroad was not a real railroad. It was a secret path. It helped slaves escape. Slaves followed these paths to the North. They used the patterns in quilts as a secret code. Each pattern had a meaning. It gave directions or a warning. Quilts helped slaves get to freedom."

Whole-Story Comprehension *(cont.)*

Directions: After you have read the story on the previous page, answer the questions below.

1. The Underground Railroad was

   a. a train car.

   b. a truck.

   c. a secret path.

2. Quilt patterns were used to

   a. keep warm.

   b. give directions.

   c. give as gifts.

3. Slaves could be free

   a. in the North.

   b. if they wanted to.

   c. when they grew up.

4. Each pattern was

   a. pretty.

   b. different.

   c. a secret code.

5. Which of the following was not put in patterns?

   a. warnings

   b. directions

   c. greetings

6. How is history like a quilt?

   a. It is soft.

   b. It is made up of pieces of stories.

   c. It is warm.

7. History changes the way we

   a. live.

   b. make things.

   c. look at the past.

8. History is

   a. stories of the past.

   b. a book.

   c. a quilt.

Enrichment

Directions: Read the information below and then rewrite each of the names. Remember to use capital letters.

A **noun** is a person, place, or thing. A **proper noun** is the name of a noun and begins with a capital letter.

Here are some examples:

The word, *girl*, is a noun.

Cindy, the name of the girl, is a proper noun.

---

1. ozella mcDaniel Williams _____

2. mrs. Johnson _____

3. dr. Sullivan _____

4. south Carolina _____

5. market street _____

Graphic Development

Directions: Look at the patterns. Create quilt patterns of your own. Then write the meaning of each pattern you make.

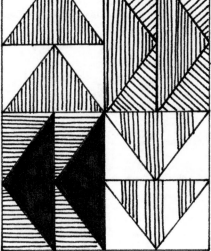

Zigzag Path

Slaves traveled in a zigzag path. They stayed away from slave catchers.

Flying Geese

Geese fly north in springtime. Slaves were reminded to head north, too.

North Star

The North Star could always be seen in the night sky. Escaped slaves used it as a guide.

Sentence Comprehension

Directions: Read the following sentences carefully and answer the questions below "True" (T) or "False" (F).

> Scientists searched inside a pyramid. They found a room. Inside they found the bones of a man.

1. All scientists look for bones. _____

2. All scientists search pyramids. _____

3. Bones were in the pyramid. _____

4. The pyramid had a room. _____

Word Study

Directions: Read the definition. Then draw pictures of two things that are shaped like a pyramid.

pyramid

a triangular form

Paragraph Comprehension

Directions: Read the paragraph below and answer the following questions.

Scientists are studying this old city. They want to know more about it.
Who built it? No one knows. Indians once thought gods built the city!

1. What are the scientists studying?

    a. Indians

    b. gods

    c. an old city

2. They want to

    a. learn more about it.

    b. live there.

    c. build a pyramid.

3. Who built the city?

    a. Indians

    b. gods

    c. no one knows

4. Do you think gods built the city?

    a. yes

    b. no

5. How will scientists learn more?

    a. They will study it.

    b. They will read about it.

    c. They will ask the Indians.

ARTICLE FROM

TIME
FOR KIDS

Name _____ Date _____

Whole-Story Comprehension

Directions: Read the story below and answer the questions on the following page.

Secrets of a Pyramid

Scientists searched inside a pyramid. They found a room. Inside they found the bones of a man. Bones of large birds and jungle cats lay nearby. Stone knives were there, too. This room is in the Pyramid of the Moon. It is in a city that is 2,000 years old. The city is called Teotihuacan (tay-o-tee-wah-cahn). It is in Mexico. It was the first great city in North America.

Scientists are studying this old city. They want to know more about it. Who built it? No one knows. Indians once thought gods built the city!

Scientists slowly unwrap the pyramid's secrets. There is much more to learn in the Pyramid of the Moon.

Name _____ Date _____

Whole-Story Comprehension *(cont.)*

Directions: After you have read the story on the previous page, answer the questions below.

1. The scientists found the bones of

   a. a man.

   b. large birds.

   c. jungle cats.

   d. all of the above

2. The Pyramid of the Moon is

   a. a planet.

   b. very old.

   c. a picture.

3. Where is the old city?

   a. India

   b. Mexico

   c. on the moon

4. Mexico is in

   a. North America.

   b. Europe.

   c. Asia.

5. Which tool was found?

   a. a gun

   b. a knife

   c. a shovel

6. A pyramid is shaped like

   a. a triangle.

   b. a square.

   c. a diamond.

7. Teotihuacan is

   a. in Mexico.

   b. 2,000 years old.

   c. both a and b

8. What will the scientists do?

   a. Sell the bones and knives.

   b. Learn more about the city.

   c. Make a movie there.

Name _____ Date _____

Enrichment

Directions: Read the information in the box below and then complete the activity. For each sentence below, draw a picture to show what it really means.

An **idiom** is a saying that means something different than what it says.

Here is an example:

Scientists slowly unwrap the pyramid's secrets.

Are the scientists really unwrapping secrets?

No. This is just a creative way to say that they are learning about the secrets.

1. It's raining cats and dogs.

2. I'm feeling under the weather.

3. There is a fork in the road.

4. Keep an eye on your sister.

Name _____ Date _____

Graphic Development

Directions: Use the map to answer the questions.

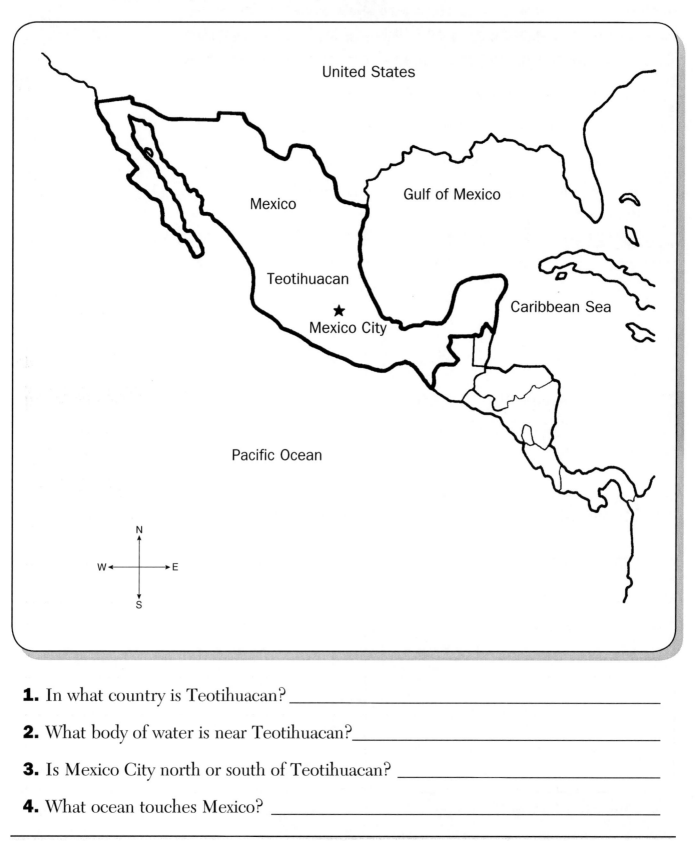

1. In what country is Teotihuacan? _____

2. What body of water is near Teotihuacan? _____

3. Is Mexico City north or south of Teotihuacan? _____

4. What ocean touches Mexico? _____

Name _____ Date _____

Sentence Comprehension

Directions: Read the following sentences carefully and answer the questions below "True" (T) or "False" (F).

> There is a rain forest in India. It is the home of the Bengal tiger.

1. India has a rain forest. _____

2. Tigers do not live in rain forests. _____

3. One kind of tiger is the Bengal tiger. _____

4. Bengal tigers live in India. _____

5. Some tigers live in rain forests. _____

Word Study

Directions: Read the information below and then answer the questions.

> The Korku are a tribe of people who live in India. A tribe is a family group. Many of the Korku live in the rain forest.

1. How do you think the Korku people live?

_____

_____

2. What do you think their homes are like?

_____

_____

3. How do you think they get their food?

_____

_____

Name _____ Date _____

Paragraph Comprehension

Directions: Read the paragraph below and answer the following questions.

> There is a rain forest in India. It is the home of the Bengal tiger. Hundreds of tigers once lived in the forest. Now there are only 70. Indian leaders want to save the tigers. They have made laws to protect the forest.

1. Years ago _____ of tigers lived in the forest.

    a. hundreds

    b. thousands

    c. lots

2. Who wants to save the tigers?

    a. visitors

    b. Indian leaders

    c. zoos

3. What did the leaders do?

    a. They trapped the tigers.

    b. They killed the tigers.

    c. They made laws to protect them.

4. How many tigers are in the forest now?

    a. 10

    b. hundreds

    c. 70

5. Why do you think the tigers are disappearing?

    a. They have been killed.

    b. They went to live somewhere else.

    c. Zoos took them away.

Name _____   Date _____

Whole-Story Comprehension

Directions: Read the story below and answer the questions on the following page.

Tigers and People Can Get Along

There is a rain forest in India. It is the home of the Bengal tiger. Hundreds of tigers once lived in the forest. Now there are only 70. Indian leaders want to save the tigers. They have made laws to protect the forest.

The Korku people also live there. They gather food and firewood in the forest. Their cattle graze there. Indian leaders want to move the Korku. They think this will protect the tigers. They will not let the Korku get wood from the forest. They will not let them get food. This will make their lives very hard.

This is wrong. People must help animals. But animals should not be treated better than people. The Korku should be able to stay. They say they will not hurt the tigers. One Korku man said, "We respect one another."

Whole-Story Comprehension (cont.)

Directions: After you have read the story on the previous page, answer the questions below.

1. Who are the Korku?

    a. leaders

    b. tigers

    c. a tribe

2. Where do the Korku live?

    a. in the city

    b. in the rain forest

    c. in America

3. The leaders say the Korku cannot

    a. work.

    b. go to school.

    c. gather wood and food from the forest.

4. Why do the leaders want to move the Korku?

    a. to protect the tigers

    b. to give them a better life

    c. to give them jobs in the city

5. Some people think that

    a. tigers are being treated better than people.

    b. the Korku are mean.

    c. the tigers should move.

6. How do the Korku feel about the tigers?

    a. They are afraid of them.

    b. They respect them.

    c. none of the above

7. The Korku want to

    a. move.

    b. kill the tigers.

    c. live with the tigers.

8. The author thinks that moving the Korku

    a. is wrong.

    b. is a good thing.

    c. needs to be done.

Name _____ Date _____

Enrichment

Directions: Read the information and then answer the questions.

The Bengal tiger is about 10 feet long. It weighs more than 400 pounds!
It is a dark orange color with black stripes. A Bengal tiger uses its color
for camouflage. This makes it hard for other animals to see it. Tigers live
alone. They need lots of space to hunt. They usually eat deer and wild
pigs. These tigers have great eyesight. They can hunt at night.

1. What does a Bengal tiger look like?

_____

_____

2. How do they keep other animals from seeing them?

_____

_____

3. What is camouflage?

_____

_____

4. Why are they able to hunt at night?

_____

_____

Graphic Development

Directions: Use the map to answer the questions.

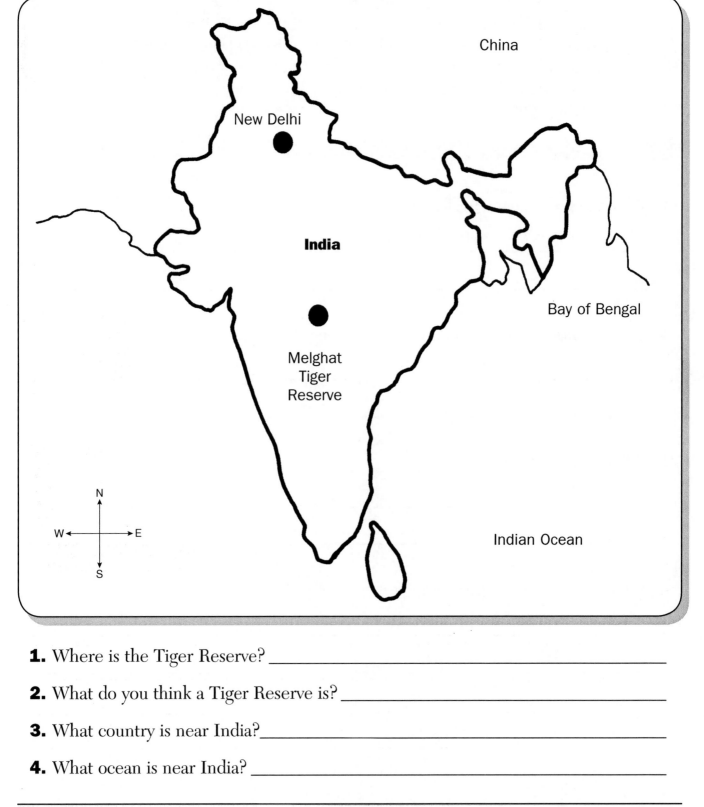

1. Where is the Tiger Reserve? _____

2. What do you think a Tiger Reserve is? _____

3. What country is near India? _____

4. What ocean is near India? _____

Sentence Comprehension

Directions: Read the following sentences carefully and answer the questions below "True" (T) or "False" (F).

> Gorillas are not mean. They are not dangerous. They eat vegetables.

1. Gorillas eat people. _____

2. Gorillas eat vegetables. _____

3. Gorillas are nice. _____

4. Gorillas are always dangerous. _____

• •

Word Study

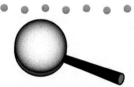

Directions: Read the definition and explain what the sentence means.

> **endangered**
>
> in danger of disappearing

Gorillas are endangered animals.

_____

_____

_____

_____

Name _____ Date _____

Paragraph Comprehension

Directions: Read the paragraph below and answer the following questions.

We must save gorillas. Gorillas are not mean. They are not dangerous.
They eat vegetables. They live in family groups. They are gentle animals.
They are also very smart.

1. A family group is probably

    a. a group that is related.

    b. several families together.

    c. a mother and a father.

2. Which of the following does not
describe a gorilla?

    a. gentle

    b. plant eater

    c. mean

3. Gorillas are not

    a. hunters.

    b. plant eaters.

    c. smart.

4. Gorilla families probably

    a. take care of each other.

    b. hurt each other.

    c. hurt people.

5. Gorillas are probably

    a. hiding from people.

    b. endangered.

    c. dangerous.

ARTICLE FROM
TIME
FOR KIDS

Name _____ Date _____

Whole-Story Comprehension

Directions: Read the letter below and answer the questions on the following page.

Save the Gorillas

Dear Editor,

We must save the gorillas.

Gorillas are not mean. They are not dangerous. They eat vegetables. They live in family groups. They are gentle animals. They are also very smart.

Gorillas live in Africa. They need a lot of room to live. Humans are taking away their land. They kill gorillas for fun. The gorillas are now in danger.

We can protect their land. We can keep humans from destroying their homes. We can stop humans from killing them. This would save the gorillas.

Please write a story about them. People need to know that the gorillas are in danger. Then maybe they will be saved.

Sincerely,

Hannah Lee

Name _____ Date _____

Whole-Story Comprehension (cont.)

Directions: After you have read the previous page, answer the questions below.

1. This letter is written to

    a. someone who works at a newspaper.

    b. a teacher.

    c. a government leader.

2. The author wants people to

    a. feed gorillas.

    b. save gorillas.

    c. have gorillas as pets.

3. Some people _____ gorillas for fun.

    a. kill

    b. take pictures of

    c. throw rocks at

4. Gorillas are in danger because

    a. people kill them.

    b. they are hiding.

    c. they don't have enough to eat.

5. We can protect gorillas by

    a. protecting their land.

    b. not killing them.

    c. both a and b

6. What does the author want the editor to do?

    a. Save the gorillas.

    b. Write a story about them.

    c. Stop killing gorillas.

7. An editor's story would be read in

    a. a book.

    b. an ad.

    c. a newspaper.

8. Who would read the editor's story?

    a. children

    b. gorillas

    c. lots of people

Enrichment

Directions: Read the information below and then answer the questions.

Gorillas live in the center of Africa. They like warm places. Gorillas are about five feet tall. A male can weigh 400 pounds.

They live in groups of five to fifteen. Each night they make beds to sleep in. Sometimes they sleep in trees.

Gorillas are smart. They have good memories. They can also solve problems.

1. How tall do gorillas grow to be?

_____

2. Where do they live?

_____

3. What do they do at night?

_____

4. How do we know that they are smart?

_____

Graphic Development

Directions: Think of an endangered animal. Plan a letter to the editor using the web below.

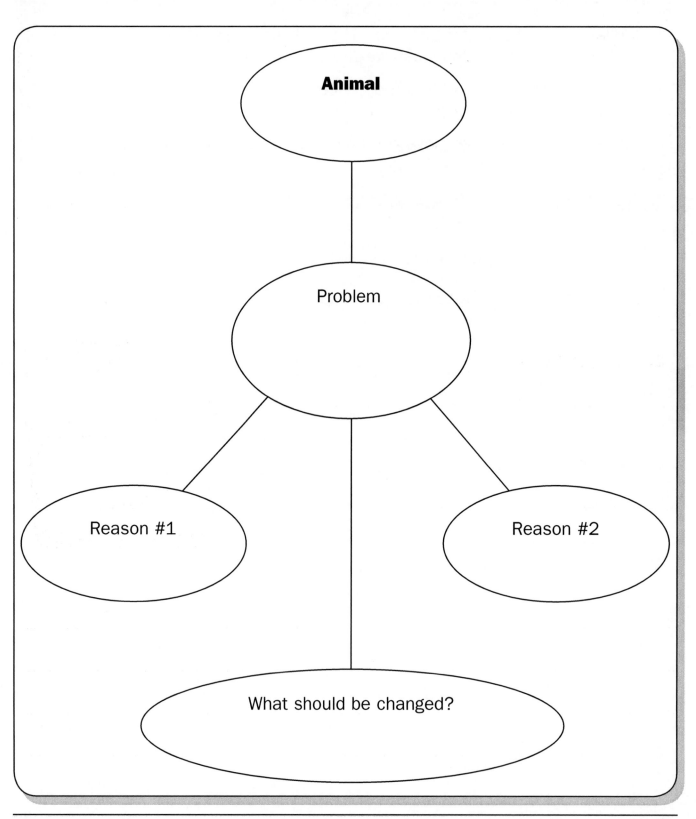

Sentence Comprehension

Directions: Read the following sentence carefully and answer the questions below "True" (T) or "False" (F).

> In 1999, nearly three million people along the East Coast had to leave their homes.

1. Many people had to leave their homes. _____

2. These people lived on the West Coast. _____

3. People live on the East Coast. _____

4. People do not build homes in the East. _____

• •

Word Study

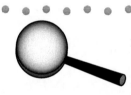

Directions: Read the definition below and then answer the question.

> **hurricane**
>
> a strong storm with heavy wind and rain that forms over the ocean

How can a hurricane be dangerous to people?

_____

_____

_____

_____

Paragraph Comprehension

Directions: Read the paragraph below and answer the following questions.

The storm began in the Atlantic Ocean. Slowly, it moved toward Florida. Then it moved up the coast. Florida didn't have much damage. But Disney World was closed for the first time ever.

1. The storm began

    a. at the coast.

    b. in Florida.

    c. in the Atlantic Ocean.

2. Why did Disney World close?

    a. No one came.

    b. There was a big storm.

    c. The rides were broken.

3. Florida didn't have

    a. much damage.

    b. people visiting.

    c. rain.

4. Florida is near

    a. the West Coast.

    b. the Atlantic Ocean.

    c. none of the above

5. A hurricane can

    a. move.

    b. cause damage.

    c. both a and b

Name _____ Date _____

Whole-Story Comprehension

Directions: Read the story below and answer the questions on the following page.

Hurricane Floyd

In 1999, nearly three million people along the East Coast had to leave their homes. Why? Because of a monster named Floyd. Hurricane Floyd was a big storm. It was 600 miles wide.

The storm began in the Atlantic Ocean. Slowly, it moved toward Florida. Then it moved up the coast. Florida didn't have much damage. But Disney World was closed for the first time ever.

All along the coast the storm left its mark. Heavy rains caused floods. A lot of things were destroyed. At least 17 people were killed.

Whole-Story Comprehension *(cont.)*

Directions: After you have read the story on the previous page, answer the questions below.

1. The story calls the hurricane

    a. a tornado.

    b. a monster.

    c. the ocean.

2. The hurricane damaged

    a. many places.

    b. Florida.

    c. nothing.

3. What happened to some people?

    a. They died.

    b. They went to Disney World.

    c. They moved to Florida.

4. What name was given to this hurricane?

    a. Fiona

    b. Floyd

    c. The Big Storm

5. What was 600 miles wide?

    a. Disney World

    b. Florida

    c. the storm

6. Hurricanes can

    a. hurt people.

    b. cause floods.

    c. both a and b

7. Why did they call the hurricane a monster?

    a. It was ugly.

    b. It had a face.

    c. It was dangerous.

8. Where did the storm go after it hit Florida?

    a. It went up the coast.

    b. It went back to the ocean.

    c. It disappeared.

Enrichment

Directions: Read the information below and then complete the activity.

Hurricane Names

Some hurricanes touch land. Some do not. But all hurricanes are given names. The first hurricane of the year is given a name beginning with A. The second one begins with B. Some have girl's names and some have boy's names.

---

1. How are hurricanes named?

_____

_____

2. Pretend there were seven hurricanes. Write names for them. (Remember to name them alphabetically.)

a. _____

b. _____

c. _____

d. _____

e. _____

f. _____

g. _____

Graphic Development

Directions: Look at the picture and answer the questions.

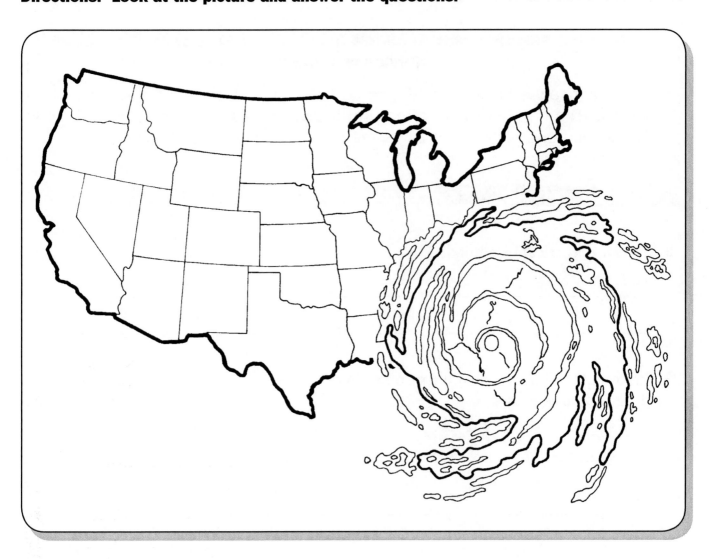

1. Look at the picture. How does a hurricane move?

_____

2. How do you think a hurricane causes damage?

_____

3. Look at the picture. Can a hurricane over the ocean still touch people on land?
How?

_____

Sentence Comprehension

Directions: Read the following sentences carefully and answer the questions below "True" (T) or "False" (F).

> The boys' dad is a dogsled racer. He has won the Iditarod twice.

1. Some people race on dogsleds. _____

2. The Iditarod is a race. _____

3. The boys' mother is a racer. _____

4. The dad has won the Iditarod three times. _____

5. The boys' dad likes to ice skate. _____

Word Study

Directions: Read the information below and answer the question.

Iditarod

The Iditarod is a sled race. It is in Alaska. Sixteen dogs pull each sled. The dogs run for many miles. It takes the racers nine to twelve days to finish. Alaska has very hard winters. The racers face deep snow. There is also bad weather. Sometimes moose damage sleds. They can hurt the dogs, too. Polar bears have even been seen. Many of the racers quit before reaching the end.

Why do you think people like to race in the Iditarod?

_____

_____

Paragraph Comprehension

Directions: Read the paragraph below and answer the following questions.

> Rohn and Nikolai Buser have a great job. They work at the Happy Trails Kennel in Big Lake, Alaska. They help train puppies.

1. Rohn and Nikolai probably

    a. don't like working.

    b. like their job.

    c. would rather be playing.

2. The boys

    a. build sleds.

    b. shovel snow.

    c. train puppies.

3. Happy Trails Kennel is a place for

    a. birds.

    b. sleds.

    c. dogs.

4. They live in

    a. a lake.

    b. California.

    c. Alaska.

5. The boys probably

    a. love dogs.

    b. take care of the dogs.

    c. both a and b

Whole-Story Comprehension

Directions: Read the story below and answer the questions on the following page.

Raising a Racer

Rohn and Nikolai Buser have a great job. They work at the Happy Trails Kennel in Big Lake, Alaska. They help train puppies.

"We don't have to do it. We like to," says Nikolai. The puppies grow up to run a race. It is called the Iditarod. It is a race that stretches 1,100 miles from Anchorage to Nome, Alaska.

The boys' dad is a dogsled racer. He has won the Iditarod twice. He wants the puppies to get lots of love. This will make them better sled dogs. His sons pet the dogs a lot. They run around with the dogs for hours every day.

Which puppy is their favorite? Nikolai says, "We like them all."

Name _____ Date _____

Directions: After you have read the story on the previous page, answer the questions below.

1. The boys are

    a. friends.

    b. neighbors.

    c. brothers.

2. When the puppies grow up they will

    a. be sold.

    b. enter dog shows.

    c. run races.

3. The boys give the puppies

    a. sled rides.

    b. lots of love.

    c. none of the above

4. The boys

    a. pet the dogs.

    b. run around with the dogs.

    c. both a and b

5. Who is the racer in the family?

    a. Nikolai

    b. their mother

    c. their father

6. The Iditarod is

    a. a kind of sled.

    b. a team of dogs.

    c. a race.

7. How many times has their dad won the race?

    a. only once

    b. twice

    c. many times

8. The boys probably

    a. wish they could be playing.

    b. would rather be inside.

    c. love their job.

Enrichment

Directions: Read the information below and complete the activity. For each item below, write a sentence using an apostrophe. Remember that sometimes the apostrophe comes before the *s* and sometimes it comes after. The first one has been done for you.

An **apostrophe** is used to show belonging.

If something belongs to one person, an apostrophe comes before the s.

For example, if a girl has a doll, we would say:

"That is the girl's doll."

If something belongs to more than one person, the apostrophe comes after the s.

For example, if a dad has two boys, we would say:

"The boys' dad is a dogsled racer."

---

1. the house that belongs to the boys

   <u>That is the boys' house.</u>

2. the car that belongs to dad

   _____

3. the game that belongs to my friends

   _____

4. the bone that belongs to the dog

   _____

5. the books that belong to the teachers

   _____

Graphic Development

Directions: Use the map to answer the questions.

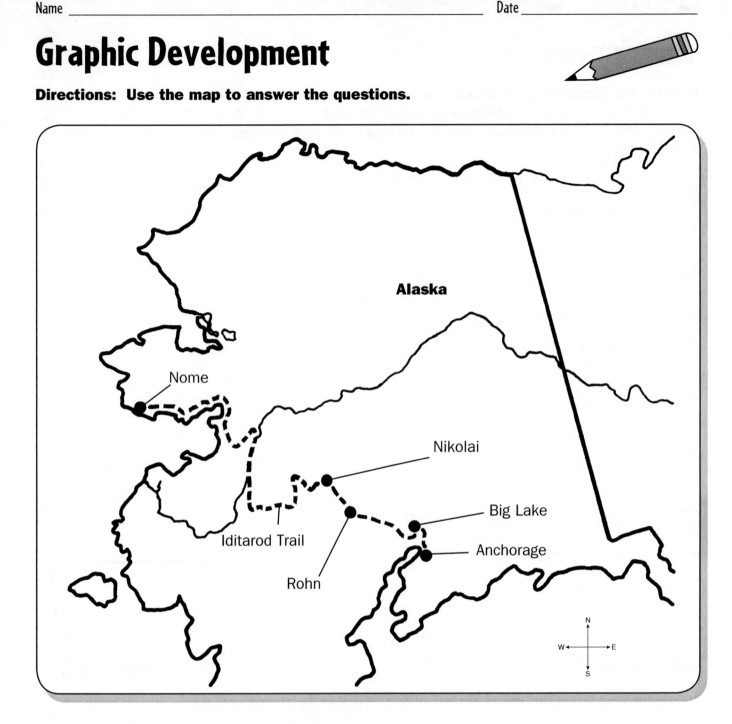

1. Which city is farther north—Anchorage or Nome? _____

2. Is Big Lake closer to Anchorage or Nome? _____

3. The boys in the story are named Rohn and Nikolai. Look at the map. What are they named after?

_____

4. Is the race path straight or crooked?_____

Sentence Comprehension

Directions: Read the following sentences carefully and answer the questions below "True" (T) or "False" (F).

> I went to my friend Jaime's birthday party. It was at the zoo.

1. The child went to a party. _____

2. The party was at the fair. _____

3. Jaime was the birthday boy. _____

4. The author of this story is a friend of Jaime's. _____

Word Study

Directions: Read the definition and answer the questions.

> **habitat**
>
> the place where something naturally lives

1. Do animals naturally live in zoos? _____

2. Many zoos call the animals' homes habitats. What do you think their homes at the zoo are like?

_____

_____

Paragraph Comprehension

Directions: Read the paragraph below and answer the following questions.

A monkey was in the next habitat. His name was Bonzo. I wanted to feed Bonzo cotton candy. My friend said, "No. That will make him sick."

1. Bonzo was

    a. a boy.

    b. a peacock.

    c. a monkey.

2. The boy wanted to feed the monkey

    a. peanuts.

    b. cotton candy.

    c. fruit.

3. What could cotton candy do to a monkey?

    a. make it hyper

    b. make it sick

    c. ruin its teeth

4. In a zoo, a habitat is

    a. an animal's home.

    b. a kind of food.

    c. a kind of animal.

5. How did the friend feel about giving cotton candy to the monkey?

    a. He thought it would be bad.

    b. He wanted to.

    c. He thought it would be okay.

Name _____ Date _____

Whole-Story Comprehension

Directions: Read the story below and answer the questions on the following page.

Don't Ever Kiss a Peacock

I went to my friend Jaime's birthday party. It was at the zoo. We saw a baby giraffe. It could run, and it was only five days old.

A monkey was in the next habitat. His name was Bonzo. I wanted to feed Bonzo cotton candy. My friend said, "No. That will make him sick."

Then we walked to a big cage. Five beautiful peacocks were inside. I wanted to see them better. I put my face very close to the cage. A peacock bit my nose! I jumped back. My nose hurt. After a second, I was okay.

Jaime's mom smiled. She said, "Don't ever kiss a peacock!"

Whole-Story Comprehension (cont.)

Directions: After you have read the story on the previous page, answer the questions below.

1. How old was the baby giraffe?

    a. a week old

    b. five days old

    c. a year old

2. What could the giraffe do?

    a. It could talk.

    b. It could do tricks.

    c. It could run.

3. What was inside the big cage?

    a. a monkey

    b. five peacocks

    c. a baby giraffe

4. Why did the boy get so close to the peacocks?

    a. He wanted to feed them.

    b. He wanted to see them better.

    c. He wanted to touch them.

5. Did the peacocks like the boy?

    a. yes, very much

    b. a little

    c. no

6. Do you think the boy will try to get close to a peacock again?

    a. probably not

    b. yes, he liked getting bit

    c. none of the above

7. The bite from the peacock probably

    a. hurt.

    b. scared him.

    c. both a and b

8. He should probably remember

    a. not to get so close to the animals.

    b. not to feed the animals at the zoo.

    c. both a and b

Enrichment

Directions: Underline the adjective in each sentence below. On the lines below write three more sentences using adjectives.

> An **adjective** is a word that describes something.

1. I went to a birthday party.

2. We saw a baby giraffe.

3. We walked to a big cage.

4. We saw beautiful peacocks inside.

5. _____

_____

6. _____

_____

7. _____

_____

Name _____ Date _____

Graphic Development

Directions: Look at the picture of the peacock and answer the questions.

1. What do the spots look like? _____

2. Why do you think a peacock has them? _____

Sentence Comprehension

Directions: Read the following sentences carefully and answer the questions below "True" (T) or "False" (F).

> The land is filled with islands and lakes. Most of it stays frozen all year.

1. All of the land is frozen all year. _____

2. This land has no islands. _____

3. Some parts of the world are always cold. _____

4. This land must be in a cold place. _____

• •

Word Study

Directions: Read the definition and explain what the sentence means.

> **territory**
>
> an area of land that belongs to a country

Canada has a new territory.

_____

_____

_____

_____

Paragraph Comprehension

Directions: Read the paragraph below and answer the following questions.

> Canada has a new territory. It is called Nunavut (Nun-a-voot). It is very big.

1. A territory is

  a. a lake.

  b. a school.

  c. land.

2. Nunavut is

  a. the name of the territory.

  b. a part of Canada.

  c. both a and b

3. The territory is

  a. big.

  b. small.

  c. out in the ocean.

4. Canada is

  a. a country.

  b. a state.

  c. a lake.

5. Who owns Nunavut?

  a. the United States

  b. Canada

  c. no one

Name _____ Date _____

Whole-Story Comprehension

Directions: Read the story below and answer the questions on the following page.

A Land of Their Own

Canada has a new territory. It is called Nunavut (Nun-a-voot). It is very big.

Most of the people who live there are Inuit. Nunavut means "our land" in their language. Inuit have lived in this place for thousands of years. Now they can really call their land "home."

The land is filled with lakes and islands. Most of it stays frozen all year. The icy land goes to the top of the world.

Nunavut doesn't have many people. There are only 28 villages. The biggest has 4,000 people.

Whole-Story Comprehension *(cont.)*

Directions: After you have read the story on the previous page, answer the questions below.

1. What does *Nunavut* mean?

    a. Canada

    b. islands

    c. our land

2. Who lives in Nunavut?

    a. Canadians

    b. Inuit

    c. no one

3. The Inuit

    a. have only lived there a short time.

    b. have lived there for many, many years.

    c. want to leave Nunavut.

4. The Inuit call this land

    a. a territory.

    b. home.

    c. a bad place.

5. Nunavut is always

    a. cold.

    b. green.

    c. warm.

6. There are _____ villages.

    a. no

    b. only 28

    c. hundreds of

7. Nunavut does not have many

    a. animals.

    b. plants.

    c. people.

8. The Inuit are probably

    a. happy to have their own land.

    b. wanting to leave Canada.

    c. wanting to build big cities.

Name _____ Date _____

Enrichment

Directions: Read the information and answer the questions.

> ### Inuit People
>
> The Inuit are a tribe of people. They live in the North. They live by the water in Greenland, Canada, Alaska, and Siberia. People used to call them Eskimos. They like to be called Inuit.

1. What do you think the Inuit do for food?

_____

_____

2. What is the weather usually like where the Inuit live?

_____

_____

3. Do the Inuit like to be called Eskimos?

_____

_____

4. What is a tribe?

_____

_____

Name _____ Date _____

Graphic Development

Directions: Use the map to answer the questions.

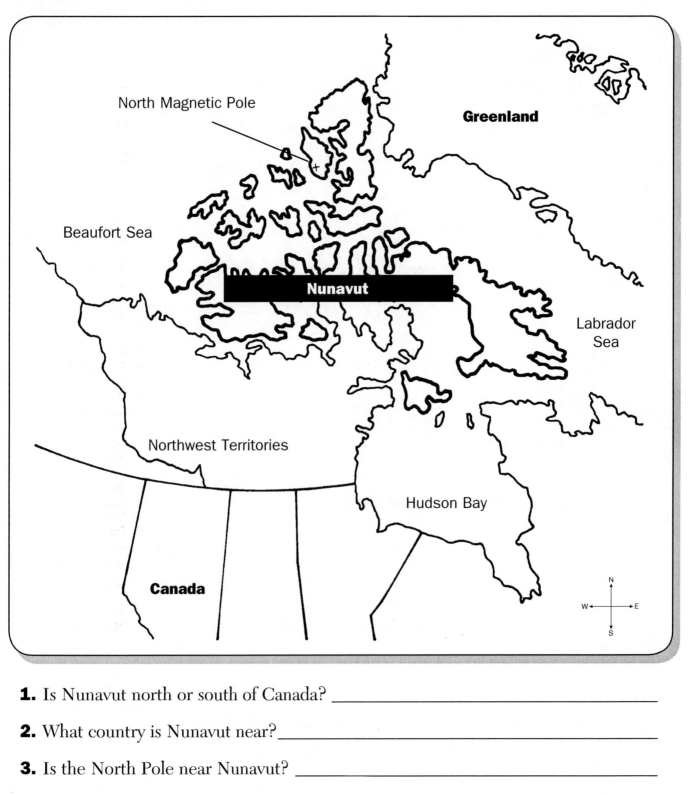

1. Is Nunavut north or south of Canada? _____

2. What country is Nunavut near?_____

3. Is the North Pole near Nunavut? _____

4. What are the names of two seas nearby? _____

Answer Key

Lesson 1

Page 21
Sentence Comprehension
1. T   4. F
2. T   5. T
3. T

Word Study
Inupiat

Page 22
Paragraph Comprehension
1. b
2. b
3. a
4. d
5. Answers will vary.

Page 24
Whole Story Comprehension
1. c   5. b
2. a   6. d
3. b   7. a
4. c   8. c

Page 25
Enrichment
1. They share food.
2. They hunt.
3. The girls learn to sew and cook.
4. Answers will vary.
5. Answers will vary.

Page 26
Graphic Development
1. T   4. T
2. F   5. F
3. T

Lesson 2

Page 27
Sentence Comprehension
1. T   4. T
2. F   5. F
3. T

Word Study
Answers will vary.

Page 28
Paragraph Comprehension
1. a   4. c
2. b   5. a
3. c

Page 30
Whole Story Comprehension
1. a   5. a
2. c   6. b
3. c   7. b
4. b   8. d

Page 31
Enrichment
1. surprise or excitement
2. excitement
3. anger
4. anger
5. excitement
6. surprise

Page 32
Graphic Development
What places has she been to?
16 countries; schools
What does she do? *She writes* Magic Tree House *books; visits schools; meets kids*
From where does she get her ideas? *kids*
Who are the characters in her books? *Jack and Annie*

Lesson 3

Page 33
Sentence Comprehension
1. F   4. T
2. T   5. T
3. T

Word Study
c

Page 34
Paragraph Comprehension
1. d   4. b
2. c   5. c
3. a

Page 36
Whole Story Comprehension
1. b   5. d
2. b   6. b
3. a   7. c
4. d   8. d

Page 37
Enrichment
1. crabs, tuna, fish
2. They are thrown on the beach; they get tired fighting waves.
3. thousands

Page 38
Graphic Development
1. coronet
2. pectoral fin
3. eye
4. dorsal fin
5. pouch
6. tail

Lesson 4

Page 39
Sentence Comprehension
1. F   4. T
2. T   5. F
3. T

Word Study
1. to get to warmer weather
2. Mexico or California
3. to lay eggs

Page 40
Paragraph Comprehension
1. b   4. a
2. c   5. b
3. c

Page 42
Whole Story Comprehension
1. d   5. c
2. b   6. a
3. a   7. c
4. b   8. a

Page 43
Enrichment
same: wings, antennae, eyes, spots, lines, etc.
different: wing shape, number of antennae, number of spots, etc.

Page 44
Graphic Development
a. 2   c. 4
b. 1   d. 3

Lesson 5

Page 45
Sentence Comprehension
1. F   4. T
2. T   5. F
3. T

Word Study
1. no   4. no
2. yes   5. yes
3. no

Page 46
Paragraph Comprehension
1. d   4. b
2. a   5. a
3. a

Page 48
Whole Story Comprehension
1. b   5. d
2. b   6. a
3. a   7. b
4. c   8. b

Page 49
Enrichment
Answers will vary.

Page 50
Graphic Development
Answers will vary.

Lesson 6

Page 51
Sentence Comprehension
1. F   4. T
2. T   5. F
3. T

Word Study
1. A   4. A
2. B   5. B
3. A   6. B

Page 52
Paragraph Comprehension
1. c   4. c
2. b   5. a
3. a

Page 54
Whole Story Comprehension
1. b   5. a
2. a   6. c
3. c   7. b
4. b   8. b

Page 55
Enrichment
1. opinion
2. fact
3. fact
4. opinion
5. fact
6. fact
7. fact
8. fact

Page 56
Graphic Development
1. long-nosed bat
2. horseshoe bat
3. tube-nosed bat
4. hog-nosed bat
5. sword-nosed bat
6. leaf-nosed bat

Lesson 7

Page 57
Sentence Comprehension
1. T   4. T
2. T   5. F
3. T

Word Study
1. reptile
2. Answers will vary.

Answer Key (cont.)

Page 58
Paragraph Comprehension
1. c   4. a
2. a   5. a
3. c

Page 60
Whole Story Comprehension
1. a   5. c
2. c   6. b
3. a   7. b
4. a   8. c

Page 61
Enrichment
1. Answers will vary.
2. prosauropod

Page 62
Graphic Development
1. Indian Ocean
2. east
3. south
4. Atlantic Ocean

Lesson 8
Page 63
Sentence Comprehension
1. T   4. T
2. T   5. F
3. T
Word Study
Nature is left alone, and animals and plants are protected.

Page 64
Paragraph Comprehension
1. b   4. c
2. a   5. a
3. c

Page 66
Whole Story Comprehension
1. a   5. b
2. c   6. a
3. c   7. a
4. a   8. a

Page 67
Enrichment
1. sometimes
2. outside
3. everyone
4. Yellowstone
5. today
6.–8. Answers will vary.

Page 68
Graphic Development
1. 21 miles
2. 30 miles

3. any two of the following: Grant Village, West Thumb, Bridge Bay, Lake, Fishing Bridge
4. about 43 miles
5. Answers will vary depending on the path taken.

Lesson 9
Page 69
Sentence Comprehension
1. T   4. T
2. F   5. F
3. F
Word Study
1. Franck Goddio—person
2. Egypt—place
3. Cleopatra—person

Page 70
Paragraph Comprehension
1. a   4. a
2. b   5. b
3. c

Page 72
Whole Story Comprehension
1. c   5. b
2. a   6. a
3. a   7. b
4. c   8. c

Page 73
Enrichment
1. no
2. the president
3. voting/an election
4. no

Page 74
Graphic Development
1. Africa
2. Egypt
3. the north
4. the Mediterranean Sea

Lesson 10
Page 75
Sentence Comprehension
1. F   4. T
2. T   5. T
3. T
Word Study
Answers will vary.

Page 76
Paragraph Comprehension
1. a   4. b

2. c   5. c
3. b

Page 78
Whole Story Comprehension
1. a   5. c
2. c   6. a
3. b   7. b
4. c   8. a

Page 79
Enrichment
1. greeting
2. message
3. closing

Page 80
Graphic Development
Answers will vary.

Lesson 11
Page 81
Sentence Comprehension
1. T   4. F
2. T   5. T
3. F
Word Study
1. A   3. B
2. A   4. B

Page 82
Paragraph Comprehension
1. c   4. a
2. c   5. b
3. a

Page 84
Whole Story Comprehension
1. c   5. a
2. c   6. c
3. b   7. b
4. b   8. c

Page 85
Enrichment
1. Your friend,
2. Fondly,
3. Your daughter,
4. Sincerely yours,
5. Yours truly,
6. Truly yours,

Page 86
Graphic Development
Answers will vary.

Lesson 12
Page 87
Sentence Comprehension
1. F   4. T
2. T   5. F
3. T

Word Study
1. B   3. A
2. A   4. C

Page 88
Paragraph Comprehension
1. c   4. c
2. a   5. a
3. b

Page 90
Whole Story Comprehension
1. c   5. c
2. c   6. a
3. c   7. a
4. b   8. a

Page 91
Enrichment
1. 400
2. three
3. five
4. 100

Page 92
Graphic Development
1. Atlantic Ocean
2. Answers will vary.
3. North Carolina

Lesson 13
Page 93
Sentence Comprehension
1. T   3. F
2. F   4. T
Word Study
Answers will vary.

Page 94
Paragraph Comprehension
1. b   4. c
2. c   5. a
3. a

Page 96
Whole Story Comprehension
1. c   5. c
2. b   6. b
3. a   7. c
4. c   8. a

Page 97
Enrichment
1. Ozella McDaniel Williams
2. Mrs. Johnson
3. Dr. Sullivan
4. South Carolina
5. Market Street

Page 98
Graphic Development
Answers will vary.

Answer Key *(cont.)*

Lesson 14

Page 99
Sentence Comprehension
1. F   3. T
2. F   4. T

Word Study
Answers will vary.

Page 100
Paragraph Comprehension
1. c   4. a or b
2. a   5. a
3. c

Page 102
Whole Story Comprehension
1. d   5. b
2. b   6. a
3. b   7. c
4. a   8. b

Page 103
Enrichment
Answers will vary.

Page 104
Graphic Development
1. Mexico
2. Gulf of Mexico or Pacific Ocean
3. south
4. Pacific Ocean

Lesson 15

Page 105
Sentence Comprehension
1. T   4. T
2. F   5. T
3. T

Word Study
Answers will vary.

Page 106
Paragraph Comprehension
1. a   4. c
2. b   5. a
3. c

Page 108
Whole Story Comprehension
1. c   5. a
2. b   6. b
3. c   7. c
4. a   8. a

Page 109
Enrichment
1. orange with black stripes
2. camouflage
3. color that keeps other animals from seeing them
4. good eyesight

Page 110
Graphic Development
1. in the middle of India
2. Answers will vary.
3. China
4. Indian Ocean

Lesson 16

Page 111
Sentence Comprehension
1. F   3. T
2. T   4. F

Word Study
There may not be any more gorillas someday.

Page 112
Paragraph Comprehension
1. a   4. a
2. c   5. b
3. a

Page 114
Whole Story Comprehension
1. a   5. c
2. b   6. b
3. a   7. c
4. a   8. c

Page 115
Enrichment
1. five feet
2. Africa
3. make beds; sleep
4. good memory/solve problems

Page 116
Graphic Development
Answers will vary.

Lesson 17

Page 117
Sentence Comprehension
1. T   3. T
2. F   4. F

Word Study
Answers will vary.

Page 118
Paragraph Comprehension
1. c   4. b
2. b   5. c
3. a

Page 120
Whole Story Comprehension
1. b   5. c
2. a   6. c
3. a   7. c
4. b   8. a

Page 121
Enrichment
1. Names are given in alphabetical order.
2. Answers will vary.

Page 122
Graphic Development
Answers will vary.

Lesson 18

Page 123
Sentence Comprehension
1. T   4. F
2. T   5. F
3. F

Word Study
Answers will vary.

Page 124
Paragraph Comprehension
1. b   4. c
2. c   5. c
3. c

Page 126
Whole Story Comprehension
1. c   5. c
2. c   6. c
3. b   7. b
4. c   8. c

Page 127
Enrichment
Answers will include:
1. boys' house
2. dad's car
3. friends' game
4. dog's bone
5. teachers' books

Page 128
Graphic Development
1. Nome
2. Anchorage
3. cities
4. crooked

Lesson 19

Page 129
Sentence Comprehension
1. T   3. T
2. F   4. T

Word Study
1. no
2. Answers will vary.

Page 130
Paragraph Comprehension
1. c   4. a
2. b   5. a
3. b

Page 132
Whole Story Comprehension
1. b   5. c
2. c   6. a
3. b   7. c
4. b   8. c

Page 133
Enrichment
1. birthday
2. baby
3. big
4. beautiful
5.–7. Answers will vary.

Page 134
Graphic Development
Answers will vary.

Lesson 20

Page 135
Sentence Comprehension
1. F   3. T
2. F   4. T

Word Study
Canada has new land.

Page 136
Paragraph Comprehension
1. c   4. a
2. c   5. b
3. a

Page 138
Whole Story Comprehension
1. c   5. a
2. b   6. b
3. b   7. c
4. b   8. a

Page 139
Enrichment
1. Answers will vary.
2. cold
3. no
4. a family group

Page 140
Graphic Development
1. north
2. Greenland
3. yes
4. Beaufort and Labrador

Answer Sheet

Directions: Fill in the bubble of the correct answer "a," "b," "c," "d," or "e" on this sheet. If the answer is "True," fill in the "a" bubble, and if the answer is "False," fill in the "b" bubble.

T F   T F   T F   T F